T0362959

PUBLISHED BY BOOM BOOKS

boombooks.biz

ABOUT THIS SERIES

.... But after that, I realised that I knew very little about these parents of mine. They had been born about the start of the Twentieth Century, and they died in 1970 and 1980. For their last 50 years, I was old enough to speak with a bit of sense.

I could have talked to them a lot about their lives. I could have found out about the times they lived in. But I did not. I know almost nothing about them really. Their courtship? Working in the pits? The Lock-out in the Depression? Losing their second child? Being dusted as a miner? The shootings at Rothbury? My uncles killed in the War? Love on the dole? There were hundreds, thousands of questions that I would now like to ask them. But, alas, I can't. It's too late.

Thus, prompted by my guilt, I resolved to write these books. They describe happenings that affected people, real people. The whole series is, to coin a modern phrase, designed to push your buttons, to make you remember and wonder at things forgotten. The books might just let nostalgia see the light of day, so that oldies and youngies will talk about the past and re-discover a heritage otherwise forgotten. Hopefully, they will spark discussions between generations, and foster the asking and answering of questions that should not remain unanswered.

BORN IN 1965?

WHAT ELSE HAPPENED?

RON WILLIAMS

AUSTRALIAN SOCIAL HISTORY

BOOK 27 IN A SERIES OF 35
FROM 1939 to 1973

War Babies Years (1939 to 1945):   7 Titles

Baby Boom Years (1946 to 1960):   15 Titles

Post Boom Years (1961 to 1970):   13 Titles

BOOM, BOOM BABY, BOOM

BORN IN 1965? WHAT ELSE HAPPENED?

Published by Boom Books

Wickham, NSW, Australia

Web: www.boombooks.biz

Email: jen@boombooks.biz

Creator: Williams, Ron, 1934- author.

Title: Born in 1965? : what else happened?

ISBN: 9780648651178

Subjects:Australia--History--Miscellanea--20th century.

Cover image: National Archives of Australia.

A1200, L52367 Australian drover;

A1200, L50213 Judith Wright, Australian poet;

A1200, L50436 Suburban back yard scene;

A1200, L50070 Teenagers on beach listening to transistor.

CONTENTS

NAMES AND FACTS YOU MIGHT NEED

Queen Elizabeth II	Queen of England
Robert Menzies	Prime Minister of Oz
Arthur Calwell	Leader of Opposition
Pope Paul VI	The Pope
Lyndon Johnston	US President
Harold Wilson	PM of Britain

Winners of the Ashes:

1962-3	Drawn 1 – 1
1964	Australia 1 – 0
1965-66	Drawn 1 - 1

Melbourne Cup Winners:

1964	Polo Prince
1965	Light Fingers
1966	Galilee

Sydney to Hobart Yacht Race:

1965	Stormvogel

Winners of Davis Cup:

1965	Australia
1966	Australia

PREFACE TO THIS SERIES: 1939 TO 1965

This book is the **27ᵗʰ** in a series of **28** books that I aim to publish. It tells a story about a number of important or newsworthy events that happened in 1965. The series will cover each of the years from 1939 to 1973, for a total of 35 books, which should just about bring me to the end of my thoroughly undistinguished writing career.

I developed my interest in writing these books a few years ago at a time when my children entered their teens. My own teens started in 1947, and I started trying to remember what had happened to me then. I thought of the big events first, like Saturday afternoon at the pictures, and cricket in the back yard, and the wonderful fun of going to Maitland on the train for school each day. Then I recalled some of the not-so-good things. I was an altar boy, and that meant three or four Masses a week. I might have thought I loved God at that stage, but I really hated his Masses. And the schoolboy bullies, like Greg Farnell, and the hapless Freddie Evens. Yet, to compensate for these, there was always the beautiful, black-headed, blue-sailor-suited June Brown, who I was allowed to worship from a distance.

I also thought about my parents. Most of the major events that I lived through came to mind readily. But after that, I realised that I really knew very little about these parents of mine. They had been born about the start of the Twentieth Century, and they died in 1970 and 1980. For their last 20 years, I was old enough to speak with a bit of sense. I could have talked to them a lot about their lives. I could have found out about the times they lived in. But I did not. I know almost nothing about them really. Their courtship? Working in the pits? The Lock-out in the Depression? Losing their second child? Being dusted as a miner? The shootings at Rothbury? My uncles killed in the

War? There were hundreds, thousands of questions that I would now like to ask them. But, alas, I can't. It's too late.

Thus, prompted by my guilt, I resolved to write these books. They describe happenings that affected people, real people. In **1965,** there is some coverage of international affairs, but a lot more on social events within Australia. This book, and the whole series is, to coin a modern phrase, designed to push the reader's buttons, to make you remember and wonder at things not remembered. The books might just let nostalgia see the light of day, so that oldies and youngies will talk about the past and re-discover a heritage otherwise forgotten. Hopefully, they will spark discussions between generations, and foster the asking and the answering of questions that should not remain unanswered.

The sources of my material. I was born in 1934, so that I can remember well a great deal of what went on around me from 1940 onwards. But of course, the bulk of this book's material came from research. That means that I spent many hours in front of a computer reading electronic versions of newspapers, magazines, Hansard, Ministers' Press releases and the like. My task was to sift out, **day-by-day**, those stories and events that would be of interest to the most readers. Then I supplemented these with materials from books, broadcasts, memoirs, biographies, government reports and statistics. And I talked to old-timers, one-on-one, and in organised groups, and to Baby Boomers about their recollections. People with stories to tell come out of the woodwork, and talk no end about the tragic and funny and commonplace events that have shaped their lives.

The presentation of each book. For each year covered, the end result is a collection of short Chapters on many of the topics that concerned ordinary people in that year. I think I have covered most of the major issues that people then were interested in. On the other hand, in some cases I have dwelt a little on minor frivolous matters, perhaps to the detriment of more sober considerations. Still, in the long run, this makes the book more readable, and hopefully it will convey adequately the spirit of the times.

Each of the books is mainly Sydney based, but I have been deliberately national in outlook, so that readers elsewhere will feel comfortable that I am talking about matters that affected them personally. After all, wharfies and strikes and the new contraceptive pill involved **all** Australians, and other issues, such as problems overseas, had no State component in them. Overall, I expect I can make you wonder, remember, rage and giggle equally, no matter where you hail from.

WHAT HAPPENED LAST YEAR, IN 1964?

If you were a **white** child born on New Year's Day, 1965, it would not have taken you long to realise that this country was a pretty good place to be in. After a week or two of reading the newspapers, you would have seen that most of the problems of the world had so far passed us by, crossed fingers. If your Dad, and perhaps your Mum, wanted work, they could get it. If your family fancied a home, say a cottage or a flat, they could dress themselves in their Sunday Best, and prostrate themselves before a bank manager. After they had done this a couple of times, he would give them a mortgage and, beyond that, the dwelling was easy.

Likewise a car was within financial reach, furniture was accumulated gradually, a TV set was affordable, and of course the Victa and Hills Hoist completed the picture. That **did** leave the average family with a big debt, including an expensive Hire Purchase commitment, but wages were reasonable, and inflation was doing its bit to ease the burden. As you would have seen from the cot, things were not too bad at all.

You might not have fully agreed if you were Aboriginal. Then, the chance of you or your mother dying at your birth would have been much increased. There was a greater chance that you would have been born with a deformity or a disease. If you were born in a hospital, a fairly small chance, you would probably **not** have gone home to a decent house, but instead most likely to a humpy and poverty. Your father would have been poorly educated, and in a low-paying job. And you and he would have had a life expectancy twenty years less than a white man. Your education would have been poor, and your status in the white-mans' community would have been low.

The **white population had just started to realise some of these terrible disadvantages**. Later in this decade, in a few States and in the Commonwealth, legislation was passed that extended voting and citizenship rights to you and your family. This of course was welcome, but in 1965 many whites still had an attitude that Aborigines were inferior, and you would face great prejudice and injustice throughout your life.

There were a few other citizens who were facing similar disadvantages. They included New Guinea natives and Asian immigrants but these, like the Aborigines, were not very vocal in pressing for reforms. Women collectively were starting to feel their oats, and the Pill was starting to provide a nicer, new freedom for some of them. Again though, at the moment they were protesting in single voices and without the philosophical leadership that would come in just a few years.

Going back, though, to you as a **white** infant, the world was your oyster. There was a celebrated writer, Donald Horne, who had just published a book called "The Lucky Country", and in it he agreed that this nation was having a good trot. Yet he also argued that **it was sheer luck on our part**, and that when things got bad, then there was doubt about whether our luck would carry us through.

That was **not the attitude of the average Aussie**. He was inclined **to doubt that things would ever get so tough**, and he was quite confident to say, in his own laid-back style, that of course we had the resilience to do whatever was called for.

But life isn't always as predictable as that, and I suggest you don't gloat too much just yet. As you will see, there might well be some **hiccups** ahead as we work our way across the year.

WHAT SORT OF HICCUPS?

Right around the globe, black and coloured people were fighting for a better deal. The blacks, or negroes, in America sought relief from a complex system of discrimination, at the same time as the blacks in South Africa were fighting for the end of apartheid. Blacks all over Africa were literally up in arms against the white colonialists who were still manipulating them, and the coloureds in South East Asia were looking to Communism to help them to full independence from their previous oppressors.

The violence that emanated from these movements was largely ignored by the Australian masses. It was all a long way off, and it seemed to come and go, and it was not at all certain that we could change anything anyway. Don't worry about it, mate. She'll be right.

Sadly, in late 1964 a situation was developing that this nation could not ignore. The world forces of Capitalism and Communism, with their incredibly short memory spans, were forgetful of the lessons from the Korean War, and were whipping themselves into a state of mutual aggression again. So America was gradually finding more examples of outrageous behaviour by the Chinese Reds, and the Reds were equally good at vilifying the Yanks. This time, they were gradually homing in on Vietnam as a nice venue for a future war, and both parties, and their allies, were adding more forces to and around the likely war zone.

Australia was not immune. We had recently sent off dozens of advisers and instructors to the region round Vietnam, and had decided that we should **re-start National Service military training for selected 20-year-old men**. The Press was carrying more and more stories about how we needed to build up our armed services, and politicians were crying out for better trained, better equipped, and more troops.

In short, everything was suggesting that some sort of major conflict was on the cards, and that Australia would not be able to simply turn a blind eye to it.

A second cause for concern for the year was our overseas trade situation. During and after WWII, our major trading partner was Britain. To that nation, we sent our wool and our wheat and our butter and mutton, and tons of other agricultural products. It was a fairly happy arrangement, with the Brits signing up for long term contracts, and quite prepared to renew, so that we had secure markets with very little marketing effort.

Now, in 1965, the Brits were starting to enter into various forms of a so-called Common Market. This was a group of half a dozen European nations who wanted to form a single trading bloc with very few tariffs between them, and generally extending trade preferences to each other. If Britain joined such a group, then she would relinquish the preferences she now gave to her Empire, and instead turn to Europe for her trading partners.

As the Brits thrashed around trying to sort out which way they would go, we in Australia had realised that the future for our overseas trade no longer lay in Britain, but in other nations closer to home. **Most prominent at the moment was Japan.** The trouble was that about half the population here still had a burning resentment against the Japanese, carried over from

WWII. This made trading with them uneasy to say the least, despite the many words from the Federal Government urging us to forgive the past.

Then there was China. It seemed to be in famine all the time, but in any case, it was prepared to buy our wheat if we were prepared to sell it to them. This, however, was always controversial. Here, ideology came into it. China was a Communist state, and we were little shadows of Capitalist America. Could we make our profits from a nation that was committed to destroy our system of Capitalism, or should we, as many people advocated, "let the buggers starve?"

OTHER INTERNATIONAL CONCERNS

Indonesia had spent the last decade getting rid of Dutch colonial influences, and trying to consolidate its many islands into a single nation. Malaya, part of the British Empire, had been doing some consolidation of its own, and now had formed a new nation, called Malaysia, that was much more independent of Britain.

These two new nations were right at each other's throats. They had some territorial disputes, and over the last year Indonesian guerrillas had infiltrated some of the islands that Malaysia controlled, and there had been some small armed clashes as a result. Both nations were pumping out the propaganda, and were threatening to attack or destroy the other. Tension was rising, and neither party was showing any sign of sense.

Australia had an interest in this in that Malaysia was part of **our** British Commonwealth. We were sending advisers, technicians, small boats, and arms to Malaya, and saying all the time that we were happy to have no interest in the potential developing brawl. But that was a silly facade, and it was clear that if the two nations did come to blows, we would intervene on behalf of the Malaysians. We need to keep on eye on that possibility.

One other matter I will briefly mention. The blacks **of the world** were revolting against their white former- masters. We **in Australia** were the dominating force over our Aborigines and the Papua New Guinea population. **They were not showing much signs of fighting to improve their positions, but we will watch carefully as we go.**

DOMESTIC POLITICS

Robert Menzies was our Prime Minister. He was head of the Liberal Party, and was very comfortable, completely unchallenged within his Party, and with a fair majority in both Houses. In his earlier years in office, he had suffered from a desire that made him anxious to change things. **Now** that zeal had gone as it always does, so he was down to sober management of the economy, and keeping one jump ahead of the Opposition. This he was doing very well.

The Labour Party Opposition was led by Arthur Calwell. He had been a Member of Parliament for two hundred years and, according to my father, had one of the most astute Labour minds of the 1850's. He was a true, old-fashioned Labour supporter, and had never become reconciled to the fact that the practice of socialism had gone out with cement horse troughs. He was struggling with a divided Party, and the chances of Labour winning any future election seemed to be zero while he remained leader.

For you, as an infant in the cot, the machinations of both political parties would readily pass you by, but for the activities of the Communists.

Communism at the time in Australia had **two faces**. The first, **the international one**, was constantly forced into our gaze by our American friends, who spent much of their energy trying to prove that their Capitalist system was superior in every way to the Communism of Russia or China. We in Australia were awash with the propaganda that this effort generated, and part of Menzies' bag of tricks was to frighten us constantly with the potential terrors of the Red scourge.

The other face of Communism in Australia that was visible was in our Trade Unions. Many, in fact most, of our Unions were controlled by Communists. This **was not, in general, because the workers were in favour of international Communism**, but rather because the local Reds were well organised, and prepared to go out on a limb against the perceived vices of the local bosses. These activists thought that the strike weapon was the right one to use, and so the nation was always plagued by tons of impromptu strikes. Menzies was annoyed by these strikes, but that did not stop him from exploiting them. He could condemn them to the full as damaging our national economy, and at the same time he could point out that this was part of the Red strategy to conquer the world by internal subversion.

So, for you, in the crib, what you will see is a very irritated mother, frustrated time and again by petty, sudden, pointless strikes, called by silly union officials, some of whom think that they are hastening along the path to a revolution that no one wants. You should forgive your Mum if your milk gets a little curdled at times. She is just responding normally to the random denial of the basics, like light, heat, all sorts of food, milk, and public transport. She is entitled to be cross.

A NOTE ON MY PRESENTATION

In this book, I rely a lot on re-producing Letters from the newspapers. Whenever I do this, I put the text in a different font, and indent it a little, and make the font somewhat smaller. **I do not edit the text at all**. I do not correct spelling or grammar, and if the text gets at all garbled, I do not correct it. It's just as it was seen in the Papers.

SECOND NOTE. The material for this book, when it comes from newspapers, is reported as it was seen at the time. If the benefit of hindsight over the years changes things, then I **might** record that in my **Comments**. The info reported thus reflects matters **as they were seen in 1965**.

THIRD NOTE. Let me apologise to anyone I might offend. In a work such as this, it is certain some people will think I got some things wrong. I am certain I did, but please remember, all of this is **only my opinion**. And really, **my opinion does not matter one little bit in the scheme of things. I hope you will say "silly old bugger", and shrug your shoulders and read on.**

OFF WE GO

So now you are ready to go straight into 1965. I hope you survive it really well

JANUARY NEWS ITEMS

In **New Guinea, patrol officers fired into 100 heavily-armed and charging natives last week,** and wounded 14 with buckshot. These natives, brandishing spears, bows and arrows, throwing-sticks and clubs, were on the point of attacking warriors from the Kewa tribe on the Fly River. **Australia,** under a mandate from the United Nations, **is responsible for law and order, and much else, in New Guinea.**

December 31ˢᵗ, 1964. Donald Campbell, from England, **set a new water speed record** in his hydroplane Bluebird on Lake Dumbleyung in Western Australia. He reached a **speed of 276 miles per hour.** Last year, he set the **land** speed record of 403 on Lake Eyre. **He is the first person to establish both records in the one year.**

The ferry service across Sydney Harbour to Manly currently takes **40 minutes. Australia's first hydrofoil** has arrived in the country, and **will cut the time to 16 minutes**.

A Staff Correspondent for the Sydney Morning Herald (*SMH*) points out that the **parliamentary Assembly in Papua New Guinea** has considerable translation difficulties. **Four languages are recognised.** They are Pidgin, English, Police Motu and Huri. Translation services must cater for all combinations, because **representatives can speak in the language of their preference.**

January 2ⁿᵈ. Britain is sending four minesweepers, a battalion of Scottish guards, one battalion of paratroopers and one of Ghurkas to Malaysia, because of the **increasing number of Indonesian landings on Malaysian territory.**

48,000 people were killed on America's roads last year. Think about it.

A new export industry was being born. Two companies, operating at Mount Goldsworthy and Hammersley, were on the point **of closing deals with Japan and also Europe for the supply of large amounts of iron ore.**

January 8th. President Sukarno, of Indonesia, announced that **his country had withdrawn from membership of the United Nations.** The reason was because the UN was supporting Malaysia in its arguments with Indonesia….

Such a move was worrying for some, because **the League of Nations had collapsed after various nations withdrew** for sundry reasons. **Would history repeat itself?**

Professor Judith Robinson got a good deal of Press coverage with **her claims that "a woman's place is not just in the home." Robinson was starting to press for a different role for women.**

The Federal Government announced at the end of last year that, due to worries over Indonesia and South Vietnam, **National Service would be re-introduced for 20-year-old males.** This meant that, apart from those exempted, males of that age would need to register, and then after a ballot, those selected would need to **spend two years in the military….**

It now said that **males must register next week,** and the ballot would be such that birthdays would be drawn at random. **Anyone born on those days drawn out would be forced to do the Service.** Their training will start in July.

Dawn Fraser was chosen by the Australia Day Council as the Australian of the Year. This followed her exploits in Tokyo in 1964 which included winning a gold medal for the third Olympic meeting in a row. She was described as "a typical unspoiled Australian girl, of unpredictable but certainly controversial reaction".

WHERE SHOULD WOMEN BE?

Judith Robinson's encouragement for women to go outside the home to find work received a lot of attention. Her timing was good, because in Australia the working load of women inside the home had been reduced by the advent of great devices like washing machines and vacuum cleaners that actually worked, crisper fabrics that required less ironing, refrigerators, electric stoves and jugs and toasters, and a cupboard-full of labour saving devices. A family car made shopping easier, and so too did the growing number of small supermarkets.

Then there was family size. Twenty years prior, there was an average of four to six children in a family. By 1965 the average size was two to three. Mum had to look after fewer children and, importantly, these children were healthier than before. In all these ways, and lots of others, the work load of the woman in the home was much smaller than before.

So when Judith Robinson spoke up about getting outside work, there were plenty of women who were happy to listen. But, as the Letters below will show, there were many different aspects to consider.

Letters, J W. Professor Judith Robinson is to be commended for urging girls to choose their career with care so that they can return to it after their children no longer require their full-time attention.

I chose a scientific career before I was married, but when I wanted to return to the workforce I found that the lack of part-time work, and my strong preference to be with my children after school and in the school holidays, turned me to school-teaching instead. But, we cannot all be school teachers just because the hours and holidays suit. Consideration will also have to be given to satisfying work being available in part-time positions.

No matter how much we would like to have 10 or 12 children, and no matter how much we deplore the present "rat race", surely it is "playing ostrich" to hanker after the Victorian days when mum did not move outside the kitchen or have time to read or discuss anything at all.

Letters, Emina Iorrisi. A woman undertaking a professional career or business life engages in a full-time occupation if she is to do it well, giving it all her talent, energy, thought and time. A woman undertaking the duties involved in caring for a husband, home and children likewise engages in a full-time occupation if she is to do that well.

It is logical, then, that no woman can do justice to two full-time occupations. Every woman is free to choose which contribution she wishes to make to society. Once she has determined her state in life, she is bound by the laws governing that particular state.

That a woman should devote her life to a career is a plausible thing. A mother, however, owes her first allegiance to her children. If she fails them, her whole life is a failure no matter whatever else she may achieve.

Letters, Egotist. Is Judith Robinson quite competent to judge whether married women with children should go to work? She has not as yet had much personal experience of the mental and physical difficulties associated with a woman leading a double life – because, after all, a man has one job and the wife who works has two. Not everyone, even with two pay packets coming in, can afford a housekeeper.

Does Professor Robinson also understand the possible side-effects on the children, even the older ones – the rush and hurry, the lack of time to talk and to listen, the feeling of being thrust into the background – as result of mother's ego? Perhaps mother may be expressing herself at the expense of others.

When it comes to understanding all this – and I think I do because I was a working mother – you realise that in life you can't always have two bites of the cherry.

Letters, Frank Avdall, Killara. Despite what Professor Robinson has to say, there are plenty of women who are as intelligent as she is, and probably more skilled in homecraft and handicrafts, who are quite content and happy to make the care of a home their full-time vocation.

Any woman who professes to manage a home and cope with a full-time job is either a liar or a genius, and there is little doubt that the present high divorce rate, slackening off of morals, and the startling upsurge of juvenile delinquency, are chiefly caused by working wives and mothers.

Letters, M Henry. It is all too easy to assume that work is necessarily the cure for women's frustrations, boredom and nerve jitters. Creative effort of some sort must certainly help, but a walk down a school corridor or two where married women can be heard, urging like harridans, leaves me in doubt about where frustration lies. Nerves, in or out of the home if caused by some deprivation of human relationship, aren't going to be solved by work alone. They may be anaesthetised, not cured.

Dr Robinson assumes, from the position of a leading academic married to an academic, that men lead such interesting lives. Many, especially among the professions do, but there are equally as many, if not more, engaged in routine pen-pushing or maybe barking their shins against the brickwall of seniority systems. To these the oasis of home freedom and make-of-the-job-what-you-will must shimmer green and inviting.

Finally, I object to being told that my duty to the community is to utilise my training this way or that way (as apparently Russian women are encouraged to do), just as I object to the dogmatic statement that "the woman's place is in the home." It is a matter for the individual to decide whether their health, sweetness of temper (and her family's), can stand two jobs, one and a half jobs, or one job – without condemnation from her fellows.

Letters, Valerie Elliston. Who will supervise the children's homework, the cuts and bruises and juvenile heartbreaks? Who will rush the family cat to the vet, when he takes on a dog he cannot handle? Who will wait at the door to hear the results of yearly exams, cricket matches and other activities? Who will veto the TV programs and organise the school vacation outings? Who will be moderator, protector and diplomat?

The answer to all these questions is, obviously, a woman, rich in tact, tolerance and patience. Where is she, this paragon of biblical virtue, for, indeed, "her price is far above rubies"? You will not find her in employment agencies. Hers is not a paid profession. She is a mother, and the measure of her success is when her children turn from her, saying: "I am now competent to make my own decisions." Only then can many women resume interrupted careers and, sadly, it is often too late.

There is no easy solution to this problem. The women are few who can afford and obtain competent domestic help. Such a woman can leave her children in another's care. Who is to say she is a **poor** mother? The children may thrive and the mother (should she be a doctor or scientist) could well pave the way to a cure for cancer. Who can measure right and wrong in circumstances such as these?

I do not know the statistics on juvenile delinquency relating to the children of working and non-working mothers, but it seems reasonable to suppose that the child who comes home from school to a kitchen full of good smells and a mother who will whack him hard on the seat of the pants if he misbehaves, is less likely to get into mischief than the child who comes home to an empty house and a key under the doormat.

Letters, R Spencer. Should I, a Government-trained BA, Dip Ed., stay at home cleaning floors and windows, sewing frocks and shirts, weeding the garden, and painting cupboards, which I at present try to do, when someone trained in these tasks could do them a lot better? These chores can surely have little effect on the love I have for husband and children (unless they make me cranky!) when they are all absent from 8.30am to 4pm.

If I had a teaching post locally, from, say, 10am to 3pm, there would be money to spare for these tasks, and by adding all the other women who are forced to remain away from teaching by present departmental policy, the staff shortage would be greatly helped.

Letters, Social Worker. It is wrong to suggest that to the choice must be career **or** home. It is possible to make a part-time contribution to a career at no expense to one's role in the family.

Because of a shortage of trained staff, I recently returned in a part-time capacity to the hospital where I was employed nine years ago. I was fortunate in being able to arrange for someone to be in the home the hours I was away so that neither my husband nor my children suffered by my absence. The sense of fulfilment and happiness I received from doing the work I enjoyed I feel sure must be reflected in my domestic life.

EDUCATION OF ABORIGINES

Australia was only just starting to recognise that it also had responsibility for the education of its Aborigines. Of course, schools had been open to them for a long time, so that it could be argued that education was freely available to them. But only now was it becoming commonly accepted that the boys and girls from this race had special problems, which needed careful and deliberate attention. The Letter below captures a little of this.

Letters, Ruth Fink. There seems a need for a more positive approach towards the education of Aboriginal children in this State. One cannot rely merely upon the goodwill and sympathy of schoolteachers who are given no special training which might enable them to understand their Aboriginal pupils better.

At present, the average schoolteacher who leaves a training college has to rely upon experience and general knowledge when he encounters an Aboriginal child in his class and often he has unknowingly absorbed some of the popular misconceptions about Aborigines, including the idea that they are intellectually inferior to white children.

At present there is no special place set aside in the teachers' training colleges for the study of Aboriginal and other minority groups and their educational problems. The only place where this is being attempted is at the Australian

School of Pacific Administration, where teachers going to Aboriginal schools in the Northern Territory and to New Guinea undergo special courses including anthropology.

Only by special training and information can we equip our teachers with a proper understanding of Aboriginal children.

This Letter stirred other writers to speak on behalf of the Aborigines. The first of these talked about the current often-accepted idea that Aborigines should be "**assimilated**" into the white population. In its most primitive form, this suggested that Aborigines should gradually, over many years, lose their own culture, and grasp hold of all of the white man's ways. **The dead opposite** to this was to say that Aborigines should maintain their own culture, and simple form ghettos remote from white influences.

Letters, J M Thomson. Suggestions for a "more positive approach" towards the education of Aboriginal children in this State have some value, but she seems to assume that it is only necessary to send out teachers armed with advice from experts and fortified with a knowledge of anthropology to have the difficulties associated with the education of Aborigines disappear.

I fear it is not going to be so simple. The education of Aborigines is so involved with problems of housing and health that I greatly doubt whether any real improvement can be brought about in it without prior improvements in the other two.

Gloria Phelan, of the NSW Teachers' Federation, has already pointed out how unrealistic it is to expect an Aboriginal child whose home lacks electric light to work by, privacy for study, books to read and perhaps even a table to do homework upon, to achieve the same educational standards as a white pupil of similar intelligence who takes all these for granted.

With State finances strained to the limit, there seems to be a distinct need for a special Commonwealth grant to the States for Aboriginal housing. Allied to the unsatisfactory housing situation in its effect upon education is an alarming, if unpublicised, health problem.

Some short time ago, there was a degree of concern expressed that the deaths of a number of Aboriginal infants may have been attributable to negligence in a country hospital. However, when a report indicated that the deaths were due to natural causes and malnutrition, there was general satisfaction that the hospital was not at fault. Few people seemed concerned that these children should have died as a result, at least partly, of malnutrition. And malnutrition is one of the factors affecting the health and education of many Aboriginal children.

It has been my experience that, in general, Aboriginal children are more susceptible than others to the various sicknesses which appear in the community and take longer to recover from them – often much longer. Cuts and sores tend to become infected and result in prolonged absences. Unsatisfactory, often non-existent, sanitation results in recurrent attacks of such things as gastritis and gastroenteritis.

Whether we wish to see assimilation or integration, there is much to be done and a great deal more money to be spent than at present is being spent before either result can be achieved, and I feel that any attempt to lift educational standards without raising housing and health standards will be unlikely to be very successful.

Not everyone was filled with such goodwill.

Letters, T Trelfoe, Nyngen. I am surprised by your correspondence on Aborigines. Any person who lives in a town with an Aboriginal population can vouch for their non-stop bad behaviour. They are not interested in assimilation or anything else, only in the gratification of primitive needs.

I do not intend to fully document their offensive behaviour, and will only remind you of their constant drinking and fighting, their delinquent children, their destruction of property including housing provided for them. What I want to do is point out that they have been like this for thousands of years, and no one will ever change that. Assimilation and any other scheme is a joke.

Comment. At this time, the above writer had many people who agreed with him. And many others disagreed.

DEATH OF WINSTON CHURCHILL

On January 25, our papers announced the death of Winston Churchill. This was the man who had led Britain through the danger years of WWII, and who had won enormous national acclaim for that. World leaders from all nations were generous in extolling his war-time performance, and our newspapers carried many Letters of affection and respect for him.

Letters, John Watson. I was standing by the York aircraft in which Sir Winston had flown from England as he disembarked at Castel Benito, the big grass airfield near Tripoli. General Montgomery stepped forward to greet him and held out his hand. Churchill grasped it in both of his hands and shook it vigorously for a long time, and this gesture, and his smile and warmth of greeting, eloquently expressed Churchill's gratitude and joy at the victory that had begun 1,500 miles back across the desert at El Alamein. It was a moment of history that will never be forgotten by those fortunate enough to see it.

Later, I was standing right alongside the wooden dais erected in the main street of Tripoli as a saluting-base for the victory march through Tripoli. Sir Winston stood there in awe-inspiring dignity and with humility as he saluted the divisions of the Eighth Army and units of the Desert Air Force. As the famous 51st Highland division, led by their pipers, surged forward, I looked at Sir Winston as he took the salute. His face was a mirror of his pride and emotion, and there were tears welling from his eyes. The tide had turned after so much "blood, sweat and tears."

That night as the sun was setting and it was almost dusk, he spoke to the headquarters staffs of the Eighth Army and the Desert Air Force. A small wooden platform had been placed in a wadi – a shallow hollow which made a small amphitheatre – and we sat around this in a semi-circle. He was dressed in Air Force uniform and had one of his big cigars sending out wreaths of smoke at frequent intervals. We were privileged to hear one of his great speeches – a speech of gratitude, faith and inspiration that included this passage:

"Let us assure you soldiers and airmen that your fellow-countrymen regard your joint work with admiration and gratitude, and that after the war when a man is asked what he did it will be quite sufficient for him to say, "I marched and fought with the Desert Army." And when history is written and all the facts are known, your feats will glow and gleam and will be the source of song and story long after those of us gathered here have passed on."

Letters, Margery Black. As a young woman in Northern Ireland, in the early 1940s, I helped in a canteen run by local ladies in a small village with a large concentration of troops.

The little old house became a rip-roaring place with the sound of heavy boots and loud voices. On special occasions the radio was switched on for a Churchill speech and then a great silence fell on these English soldiers. They stopped eating, sat perfectly still and listened intently.

This is my wartime memory of the Churchill "magic."

Letters, I Scott, Denistone. The fine poems by the Poet Laureate and George Frazer which were published in the Herald on Tuesday serve to remind us that there is a land called England and a people known as English.

The tendency, for some years, has been for the terms "England" and "English" to be superseded by "Britain" and "British." The free peoples of the world may owe their freedom in general to the British, but in particular it is to the steadfastness of England and the English led by the great Englishman Churchill that the debt is owed. The two poems emphasise this oft-forgotten truth.

Note, though, that there were some **wardrobe antagonists** to Churchill. None could be found in the Sydney newspapers, but this moderate piece below was published in the Cessnock Eagle. My experience talking to many readers of these books indicates that **he was not alone in his opinion.**

Letters, Arthur Neathy, Corrimal. Cessnock Eagle.
Churchill's funeral was marked with all the pomp and circumstance that would be expected for such a hero. Here too in Australia, homage on a broad scale was made to him. Yet there were many in Australia who quietly had thought differently about the great man.

During the war, to publicly criticise a person of Churchill's standing was risking charges of treason. So critics were thus stifled. After the war, and into 1965, criticism remained muted, and our newspapers carried no Letters that were not glowing in praise.

Critics argued that the involvement of our army in Greece and then Crete in WWII, and our huge casualties there, were a result of very **bad decisions by Churchill**. Some of the old timers add that **the Anzac fiasco** of WWI was Churchill's fault. They all remembered that John Curtin, our war-time Prime Minister, had to fight tooth and nail to get Churchill to **send our own forces back home** after the Japs came close to our shores. These critics were all of the opinion that **Churchill was careless with Australian lives.**

Churchill to me was indeed a great winner, but we would do well to remember that his faults also (probably needlessly) cost many thousands of Australian lives.

FEBRUARY NEWS ITEMS

Twenty-five people were killed and hundreds injured when panic seized **a crowd in a bullring at Mexico's second largest city.** The people were either suffocated or trampled. This is a reminder that, at Spanish-speaking cities throughout the world, bull **fighting was still a common event.**

On February 2nd, it became obvious that the Liberals, led by **Bob Menzies, had lost a recount in the recent Senate elections, and so now he will not have control of the Senate.** By the time he provides a Speaker, he will have a tied House. This will make governing much more difficult.

The Editor of the *SMH* ran an article that pointed out that **Japan's new bullet train was now running at 160 miles per hour.** Enthusiastically, he went on to describe work being done at Nagoya University that aimed to have trains run at the speed of sound. Which, I add, has never happened….

I point out that the pioneer Japanese Bullet Train has now (in 2015) doubled its speed, and **the idea has spread to all parts of the world. Except Australia.** And America. We still (2020) have "express" trains **from Sydney to Brisbane that run at an average speed of 40 miles per hour for the 600 mile journey. Whacko.**

Three men were killed, in three separate accidents, at the opening of the duck shooting season in NSW today. Two of them drowned, and the other was accidently shot.

The Duke of Edinbough, Prince Phillip, visited **Sydney for three minutes** today. He was on his way to Canberra, and his Qantas plane touched down at Sydney's Mascot terminal. He came waving down the steps, walked 6o feet, and boarded an Army Viscount jet bound for Canberra. **It was the briefest**

Royal Visit anywhere on record. **He will not be seen very much by the Australian public on this visit.**

Saturday night, February 20th. More than 350 people were arrested after **1,000 police swept** on Saturday night **on the suburban streets of Melbourne**. The aim was to eliminate the larrikinism, drunkenness and assaults on women that have plagued the suburbs recently. It was the biggest campaign since **the police "bodgie" squads** waged war on youths in the 1950's.

The Duke was taken to the Mint in Canberra, and there it was **his finger that pushed the button that started production of Australia's new decimal currency**. The coins thus made were stockpiled for a year, and then released **into circulation in February, 1966**.

A US film director, Kenneth Hume, was awarded an uncontested divorce against singer **Shirley Bassey** in London, on the grounds of her adultery with two men. One of these was Australian actor, **Peter Finch**.

Britain's Chief Justice, Lord Parker, had a thought. "If you say **a single innocent** man might hang, it raises horror. But if you say that **1,000 innocent men** will die on the roads this year, it hardly raises that flicker of an eyelid."

The Headmaster of England's Eton school shared his wisdom. "We have the same number of spoiled boys as other schools, but **our spoiled boys are much richer."**

Hire Purchase Companies advanced 35 million Pounds to customers last month for retail sales. New and used vehicles accounted for 70 per cent of this. **The total for the year was a record.** This provided confirmation of **HP's ever-increasing growth in importance in financing household debt**.

TROUBLE TO OUR NORTH

The Indonesians and Malaysia were continuing to niggle each other, and the Yanks were showing how tough they could talk in Vietnam and Laos. The game of provocation and then retaliation was escalating. Looking back, it is obvious that all the nations involved **were being conditioned** to the notion that a bigger conflict was more than likely.

For the rest of the book, I will not report these acts of mutual animosity, but ask you to remember that they are going on, day after day, and gradually getting more serious. **I will report on them only here and there, just enough to keep you up to date.**

THE END OF ANZAC MARCHES

Every year, there was a spate of Letters around Anzac Day, that said all the normal things. Some people complained about the public transport to marches that occurred across the nation. Others wanted children to march. Others did not. Some decried the boozing and two-up that followed. A few said the Diggers should have one day a year for themselves given the years and years they had spent away for home. There were always lots of other messages as well.

This year, the traditional pattern was disturbed. One Letter was published in the *SMH* that fired up lots of respondents. This was in February, and not April, but it also **took a different tack altogether.**

> **Letters, N Quigley.** As an old digger, I make a plea that **this Anzac Day march** in April, which is the 50th anniversary of the Gallipoli landing, **should be the last**.
>
> In latter years the march has become something of a burlesque, particularly in so far as **World War I** men are concerned. Some drop out after a short distance; others lead grandchildren. All the men are old in any case. We have had our run, we have had the adulation, we have had

all the perks and preferences, we are even having free fares to the march. **The image of the Digger is now one of free hand-outs, preference and perks.** As an old soldier these things are anathema to me.

As regards the 1939-45 men, only a fraction of the enlisted personnel ever saw a shot fired or served in a theatre of war. Finally, in my opinion, the Anzac march has degenerated into a beer and poker-machine bonanza. In conclusion I finally plead: **Make this the last.**

This was an unusual view. Would other writers share it? Well, Mr Buckley, of Bondi Junction did.

Letters, D Buckley. As an infantry soldier of the 1939-45 war, my memories of it are not pleasant, and Anzac Day marches only serve to remind me of that which I would rather forget. Although I am entitled to, and physically capable, of taking part in the Anzac March, I never have, and I never shall. And I am not alone when I say I do not turn on the radio on Anzac morning.

Mr Quigley is quite right when he says only a fraction of the enlisted personnel in the 1939-45 war saw a shot fired. To see men marching on Anzac Day who were never in danger at any stage of the war, and to hear the younger generation cheer and shout, scarcely knowing what it's all about, and as the day wears on, see it degenerate into boastings, booze and worse, fills me with disgust.

Let future Anzac Days be silent days of prayer, held on the nearest Sunday to April 25, and let us have no more of this carnival, this Roman holiday, for those who do not understand.

Mr Summerville weighed in with the reminder that, in Britain, Remembrance Day is a quite reverent day, whereas here it is a "beer-swilling bonanza" that "makes a mockery of remembrance". Mrs Wilson of North Sydney sees the day as "an unnecessary holiday for the underworked and overpaid workers in Australia". Whatever slant they put on it, all the above writers wanted the march to finish permanently.

Mr Faye of Bateau Bay, in a scattered Letter, was prepared to really lay in the boot. He said that "**every** old Digger **claimed** to be at Gallipoli, and **all** of them **supposedly** saw service in Cairo.... We will have much pleasure in telling him what a lying mob of no-hopers the First World War Diggers were." As to those from WWII, he describes them as "bred on beer, and bludging on the hard-earned glory of the WWI Diggers."

This was a feeling not shared by the majority. Writers flocked to say that the Diggers should have their day. I quote from just two.

Letters, N Jackson. I landed on Gallipoli as Private 118 in the 1st Battn. Infantry on April 25, 1915, and spent over seven months there and have now passed my seventieth birthday and intend to march this year and as long as I can.

I owe this little sacrifice to my dead comrades who shared the hardships with me on Gallipoli and who are buried there. The march is an inspiration to thousands of young people who line the route as onlookers, in the cities and towns of Australia, year after year and if called on, as in the last war, will carry the torch and emulate the dash and gallantry of the original Anzacs when in battle.

Mr Quigley's quip at the bonanza of booze and poker machines should be disregarded. At the reunions after the march, the toasts are drunk with beer but poker machines are conspicuous by their absence. As to Mr Quigley's handouts, I don't receive anything, not even a pension, not being eligible. But those that receive them get them only after severe tests by the Repatriation Department.

The boys that did not see a shot fired in the last war had to go anywhere the High Command ordered, but those thousands that did, acquitted themselves as blue-ribbon Anzacs, and we originals are honoured to have them carry on the March of the Anzacs on April 25. The torch is safe in their hands.

Letters, Wal Barrie. It is the absolute right of all Anzacs and World War I Diggers to have their march and day of reunion. On behalf of Diggers of World War I, I protest emphatically against the slur thrown at our World War II mates. Comparisons are odious, but I was on Gallipoli when privations were the order of the day, but I would not have liked to be in Malaya; I was in Pozieres but I would not have liked to serve on the Kokoda Trail.

Mr Quigley sounds as if he has a chip on his shoulder, and probably he was a base wallah.

Comment 1. These tough attacks on Anzacs got almost no support from the general community. They did not flow over into the other newspapers, nor did they recur in later years.

Comment 2. A few of the dissidents said disparagingly that many of our servicemen did not "see a shot fired or see a theatre of war." I simply say that not everyone can be in the front line, and that simply to take a youth or a man away from home for years on end, and to make him live under Army conditions, is a great punishment without a crime.

Comment 3. In case anyone forgets, the number of Australian males who lost their lives in WWI was over 60,000. In WWII, it was over 30,000. In both wars, the number of casualties was more than double that. Writers who suggested that many of our men "did not see a shot fired" should have checked their facts.

OZ FREEDOM RIDES

About the middle of February, a busload of students from Sydney University headed for the far west of NSW with the aim of highlighting abuses to Aborigines. This so-called "freedom ride" was emulating those in America which had been successful in bringing many gross abuses of Negroes to the attention of the wider public. Our students were not deterred by the fact that the more spectacular US rides had sometimes ended in violence, riots and even deaths.

The students went to a number of towns and sought out abuses to Aborigines. They were very easy to find. For example, in Boggabilla they found that the public housing was in a deplorable condition, and that certain pubs discriminated against the blacks. In the latter cases, they tried to get appropriate liquor trades Unions to put a black ban on those hotels.

Letters, TEACHER, Boggabilla. When I heard that the students were on their way here, I rejoiced. This town, and all the Far West, abounds with Aborigines who are discriminated against every day. I thought they would came here and soberly pin-point some problems and sensibly display them on the national stage, so that some good policy decisions would be made to fix the problems.

They did not do that. They turned out to be a publicity-drunk rabble. They wanted the headlines, and they wanted every minor situation to escalate till it became a major issue fit for the headlines.

Here in Boggabilla, they wanted to get an immediate Union ban on delivering to the pubs that discriminate against Aborigines. Let me tell you that if those pubs sell to the Aborigines, then the white patrons will go elsewhere. The point is that it is not a simple fix.

But more to the point, suppose they got a ban on a few pubs, for a few days, in Boggabilla. What would that achieve? What is needed is a national policy to carefully consider the black issue. A few rat-bags scuffling in the streets, holding a few banners, and whipping up crowds of Aborigines to violence will not help. That only diverts frivolous media attention to the banana's skin, and not to the banana itself.

The focus of the ride became the township of Moree, and the town's swimming pool. In 1955, an ordinance had been passed by Council banning full or part-blood Aborigines from the pool. This was supposedly on the basis that Aboriginal children were hygienically unsuited for the baths. In 1961, an amendment was passed allowing the children access for Wednesday school sports and for carnival days and training.

For over a week, some provocation or other stirred passions every night at the pool. It was blistering hot in the February nights in the town, and the pool attracted large numbers of swimmers. There were also dozens of newspapermen with their cameras, and a few television crews, all loitering with intent to create news. So the scene was set for drama.

For example, one night, management said it would reject "dirty" children. So it somehow managed to select the dirty ones and expelled them. On another, it let in a large number of Aborigines, but expelled many because they had no swimming clothes apparent. **The "ride" was tricky in its own way.** One night when the pool was full because of the extreme heat, the management closed the pool to new entrants. The "ride" was waiting outside with about 40 aboriginal children and then tried to enter. When they were refused, they cried discrimination, and **made the newspapers the next day.**

All the while, black and white adults in towns right across the nation were getting angry. Long-held prejudices were being aired. Many white men and women were clinging to their belief that Aborigines would only destroy any houses that might be built for them. Many whites said that blacks would be a menace in any pub under any circumstances, because they could not hold their liquor. Many said that they defecated in public pools, and that no white child should swim with them. On the other hand, the Aborigines had their supporters. Let's see what the Herald writers thought.

Letters, (Mrs) B Booth. Aren't university students wonderful? They barnstorm quickly through the country causing dissatisfaction, even minor violence, and then scuttle back to their fine, comfortable homes and leave the country townspeople to cope with the havoc they have caused.

Have any of them ever lived in a country town where Aborigines have their camps? Have they ever seen them on endowment day? Straight to the pubs for the men and straight to the chain-stores for the women – load the kids up with cheap toys, sweets, ice-cream and as much "lolly water" as they can hold!

Have any of them ever employed Aboriginal girls in their homes, and had to hold their pay for them to see that they got warm clothing for the winter and not cheap jewellery and pictures and milk shakes with all of it? Have any of them been to Yamba to see where the council has built them six new brick homes to take the place of their old humpies? I suppose they would say that discrimination is there as these homes have been built away from the town and on a lonely beach. Of course, they wouldn't take time to learn there would be no point in taking the Aboriginal away from his former site. After all, he chose it himself years ago, because it was the best place for fishing, worming and general food gathering.

These university students all seem to have plenty of money, as they are not working during their long vacation. Why don't they put their money into an endowment or scholarship for the Aborigines with brains and a sense of responsibility? There are some, you know. Take a trip to Palm Island off the coast of Queensland and see what the Aborigines can do when they are looked after by the proper authorities, who have lived and worked with them for years, and not made a 24-hour visit to make hasty decisions and pass judgment on a lot of hard-working white people who have to put up with all the strife caused by this misplaced zeal.

Letters, G W Ford, Lecturer, Economics, University of NSW, Sydney. The students who went to Walgett and Moree are not, as Mrs Booth insinuates, poor little rich kids who are bored with holidays. Some of the group are part-time students who were willing to devote a portion of their annual holidays to put their social ideals into practice. Many of the group have worked hard all vacation to get enough money to pay for the hire of the bus and their living expenses. Some of the group even went into debt to guarantee the money for the hire of the bus.

Mrs Booth claims the students should have devoted their efforts to Aboriginal scholarships. Students at Australian universities have been raising money for Aboriginal scholarships since the early 1950s and many of the riders on the Student Action for Aborigines Council bus have devoted considerable energy to this cause.

In fact, the leader of the group is an Aboriginal scholar who is at the University of Sydney because university students all over Australia raised the money for his scholarship. The SAAC group not only worked hard raising money for their tour but they spent many of the hot January nights listening to lectures on such topics as anthropology, problems of social welfare, how to conduct social surveys. The lectures were given by scholars who have in many cases devoted a lifetime to studying these problems.

Letters, G Briot. Mrs Booth righteously lists some facts about Aborigines and their behaviour.

The true facts are that the Aboriginal is a product of the degrading environment in which white men have obliged him to live. He is humiliated, pushed around and discriminated against from the day he is born, and suffers perhaps the most damaging discrimination in the educational field.

When Mrs Booth writes of students causing strife and havoc in country towns she, in fact, means that they are peaceably and legally drawing the nation's attention to a shameful state of affairs which the residents of the towns concerned attempt to keep out of sight and certainly out of mind. The present extreme discomfiture of these towns-people is a product of their own sins. The students' bus tour, in bringing forcibly to public attention that the American "deep south" has a counterpart in NSW, merits the highest commendation rather than prejudiced abuse.

Letters, (Miss) K Stanton. To Mrs Booth and to readers of her letter, I would like to give a student's opinion. The Student Action for Aborigines Council was certainly "ready to take up a cause with the greatest enthusiasm," but also with as much knowledge of the subject as possible. In order to go on the bus tour, each student had to attend seminars given by experts on "freedom rides," local government, social sciences, local health situations, anthropology, etc., and detailed reports on the position of the Aborigines in each town as well as read a lot of relevant material.

Although this organisation was formed in the last term of 1964, the students have worked hard to raise money for the tour and finding out sources of all kinds of necessary information. Charles Perkins, part-Aboriginal student leader, late last year visited a number of towns throughout the State to add more definite facts to his knowledge, and two student groups made preliminary trips to the areas to gain even more material and assess the particular situation in each town.

The students have gone with a deep concern to help the Aborigines in numerous ways differing for each town, and usually by setting up committees or helping existing ones with which they intend to work and by correcting every form of discrimination if possible.

It is not only the bans against the Aborigines which must be abolished but the reason for them, whether it is a man's ideas or a physical condition. If it is health, then we must improve the living conditions and train the Aborigines patiently. If it is from further schooling, then we must improve their study conditions and give equal pay to parents or encourage saving for the necessary finance, etc. It may interest all to know that the universities do provide Aboriginal scholarships.

I think that not working for two weeks out of three months' vacation is pretty fair and that it's jolly decent for the students to use it in helping our Aboriginal citizens and, ultimately, the country towns.

Letters, (Mrs) Lorna Firth. I think it is a very good thing that the university students are exposing the way the Aborigines are being neglected in our country towns, and no one who has visited such towns can deny that there seems to be a case for complaint against segregation.

I sincerely hope, though, that the students realise that it is not enough to bring people's attention to the wrong being done without having some concrete idea of how the wrong can be righted. It is to be hoped that these young people have a "mission" in life to go to those towns and work with and for the maltreated Aborigines. It is one thing to cry "Shame!", and another to spend months and perhaps years bringing both white and coloured people together.

For a lot of white people living in towns with a fringe of Aborigines, the latter often are unhygienic, and apparently lazy and shiftless. On the other hand, it seems that not many employers in shops, chain stores, offices, council chambers, factories, etc., try to employ coloured girls and boys from these fringes to give them a chance to show whether they must be lazy and shiftless and unhygienic or whether their environment is the cause.

Letters, Carolyn Booth. It is comforting for bigoted whites to develop a mind-picture of Aborigines as inferior in intelligence, moral worth, ability and the rest of it. The white man in the street would rather not think about the racial problem, and when he is compelled to do so conjures up the "image of a filthy, lazy, drunken 'abo'."

What can be done about this? To educate Aboriginal children to a higher standard, to indoctrinate them with our ideals of cleanliness and industry, to take them from the reserves and humpies and settle them where they could learn to become an integral part of the Australian community – this would break down one of the largest barriers to integration – so long as the supposedly superior whites act like mature and responsible human beings, rather than blinkered draught-horses, shying at a leaf.

Letters, Anti-Sham. The photograph of Aboriginal Gary Williams having a drink of beer in a hotel with student Brian Aarons is enough to make anyone vomit. Is the Aboriginal lad supposed to be uplifted by learning the great Australian grog guzzle? Now, if young Mr Aarons took the Aboriginal into the Aarons home for the weekend, that would be something?

Comment. The "ride" was a big event in Australian Aboriginal history. For all its faults, and whether you consider **it a cause or an effect of changing attitudes**, it certainly left a permanent impression. The average moderate citizen was made aware of the raw deal that was highlighted by the "ride" and, possibly for the first time, started to consider what could be done to remedy the mess.

MARCH NEWS ITEMS

Are hemlines going up? The Paris fashion designer, Jacques Esteral, makes his opinion clear. "The knee and the leg are **spiritual** things that should be seen."

Four Australian Olympic girl swimmers were expelled from the Australian Swimming Union **for periods of up to ten years. They were Dawn Fraser (10 years), Linda McGill (4 years)**, and two others for three years each. This means that **Fraser cannot swim in the next Olympics**, and will miss the next Empire games....

No reason was given for the expulsion. It was believed to be because of their conduct in the recent Olympic Games in Tokyo, and was connected to **an incident with the Japanese flag in the grounds of the Emperor's palace.** Fraser and McGill announced that they will challenge the decision in the Courts.

Sir Thomas Playford had been **Premier of South Australia continuously for 27 years**. His Party was defeated in State elections of February 6th, and **he resigned as Premier** as a consequence. March 11th.

March 11th. Two female employees were killed when **a bomb exploded in the Australian Embassy in Singapore**. It is initially thought that the bombing was the work of Indonesian saboteurs. A total of 33 other persons were injured.

Mr Ken Tall of Rockhampton was relieved of 75 Pounds for painting his name on Ayers Rock. He saw that many others had carved their names into the rock, and he thought that paint was the better medium. He was kind enough to add his address, so the long arm of the law stretched out and got him in Rockhampton. He was fined two Pounds, with 73 Pounds witness costs.

When Churchill died some weeks ago, the Federal Government announced that it was **creating a Churchill Memorial Trust** that would allow outstanding Oz students to go overseas to get post-graduate qualifications. The fund was to come from public subscription, and **the target was one million Pounds**....

On February 1st, when the Fund was due to close, the sum of 1,800,000 Pounds had been raised. By the end of the month, money was still coming in, and a **total of over two millions was in the coffers**. A fitting tribute.

On March 18th, a Russian astronaut stepped out of a space capsule orbiting the earth (at 5 miles per second), and remained outside for 10 minutes. This was a feat that no man on earth had achieved before. Millions of Russians watched the event of television.

Prayers for rain will be said in all Roman Catholic Churches until the drought breaks. The format of the prayers was not mandated. It has been suggested that Anglicans do the same, and that **the following prayer from the Anglican Book of Common Prayer is appropriate**....

Church prayers... "O God our Heavenly Father, who by Thy Son Jesus Christ has promised to all them that Thy kingdom and its righteousness, all things necessary to their bodily sustenance, send us we beseech Thee, in this our necessity, **such moderate rain and showers that we may receive the fruits of the earth** to comfort and to Thy honour, through Jesus Christ our Lord."

Do you remember Mavis Bramston?

DAWN FRASER IN JAPAN

The Emperor's Palace in Tokyo did much more than provide accommodation for the Imperial family. The edifice was regarded as a symbol of many sacred traditions for the entire nation, and was now constructed of reinforced concrete, of three floors, largely surrounded by a wide moat, and guarded 24-hours-a-day by a most aggressive army unit. When Dawn and her two colleagues breached its security and took its Olympic flag, it was not just a matter of petty theft, but a serious insult to the Japanese nation, and **a cause for diplomatic concern**.

Fraser had a reputation for larrikinism and for not complying with authority. Still, both before and after the Tokyo Olympic Games, she had enormous public support, and was already regarded as **something of a national treasure**. So when the swimming powers-that-be suspended her for ten years, public opinion was divided.

Letters, Phyl. Lynton-Smith. I hope that the majority of Australians will protest with me against the arbitrary treatment meted out to our Olympic girl swimmers. Not only have the girls themselves not had their fair say, but the details have not been given to the public. Moreover, the punishment appears to be excessive.

No appeal! Are we really in democratic Australia? The girls may seem to have behaved badly – the question is why? Were they kicking against the pricks of a too rigid discipline? If so, they acted as Australians have always done, fighting against authoritarianism and over-zealous, pettifogging officialdom.

Does any Australian really believe that the girls should have missed the opening march of the Games? If so, they miss the century-old spirit of the Olympics in which the Greeks came together in peace and goodwill to join in the sports. Too much national competition and pressured direction now threaten to destroy this original concept.

Letters, H V Howard. The public generally will endorse the action of the Australian Amateur Swimming Union in disciplining four of its members for infringement of rules at the Olympic meeting at Tokyo, in spite of a strong campaign against the ASU decision.

In recent times, contestants at Olympic Games have apparently been selected on their records alone of prowess in some particular field, without any consideration being given as to whether they can truly represent their country by their other qualities.

Our mentors, from earliest times, have endeavoured to imbue us with the idea that the attainment of success in the sporting field is most influential in building strong character. It cannot be denied that many of our representatives at Tokyo have given the lie to this ancient shibboleth.

Letters, (Mrs) J Frame. I wish to add my protest to those who are incensed at the harsh treatment of four of our top-flight swimmers.

No one denies that discipline is necessary and no one knows it better than a champion swimmer. Many long years of self-discipline, sacrifice, dedication and heavy expense go to make a swimmer of the calibre of these girls – who seek to win honour for their country as the pinnacle of their endeavour.

Discipline should not be confused with tyranny, and if the girls have rebelled against injustice and tyranny, that is a tribute to the spirit that makes them the champions they are. If competitors are to be disciplined, it should be administered by people who are competent, wise, understanding and just. The present decision, as it stands, does nothing, in my mind, to indicate that the officials are rich in these qualities.

Letters, R B C Herbert. The expulsions handed out to the Olympic swimmers is a true admission of lack of control by Australia's officials on the spot over team members, one of whom is only 15 years of age. Such drastic action, so late, is proof of their own incompetence and powers and should apply to the officials as well.

Disciplinary action should have been taken immediately in Tokyo. To have robbed a contestant of the chance to compete would have disciplined all and sundry.

Letters, Colin Rodgers. I would like to support wholeheartedly the actions of the ASU despite the outcry on behalf of Australia's female demi-god – Dawn Fraser. True, she may have won some gold medals and may have enhanced our sporting prestige – a nebulous thing in any case – but do these factors give her the right to disregard rules and do they set her above reproach.

All four swimmers were not only an example of our prowess in sport, but also our manners. People in the public eye – especially such a heroine as Dawn – must always act accordingly whether they like it or not. A true champion is signified by bearing and uprightness as well as by records.

I must admit, however, that the right of appeal being denied is unjust. But if the facts are there the penalties should be exacted.

Letters, (Mrs) Mydie McDonald. It is to be fervently hoped that the four young women swimmers expelled by the Australian Swimming Union will get full public backing in having rectified the injustice that has been placed upon them.

Any behaviour that was so gross as to merit this punishment would have been dealt with on the spot by officials of commonsense, even to the point of sending the girls home. The only elements missing from the ASU's treatment of them seem to be the stocks and the branding.

Comment. Fraser was re-instated four years later, but it was too late for her to train effectively for the 1968 Olympic games. She has gone on, through difficult years at times, to become a quixotic symbol of propriety, and has gained many honours including the OA. She remains in high esteem with the Australian public.

BIRTH CONTROL

The use of the contraceptive "pill" was growing at a rapid rate. No one was really certain that it would work all the time, or that it would continue to work. Young women who wanted to have sex, but not children, were often discouraged from using it. There were some stories circulating about how it would sooner or later produce deformed children, or induce illnesses in mothers. There were stories that it was the agent of the devil who was intent on corrupting young innocents. There were theories circulating that the population of the nation would dry up if enough women used it.

One body that produced its own scare tactics was the Catholic Church. It held that the main aim of sex in marriage was to procreate, and so that couples should restrain themselves by using the so-called rhythm method. This involved refraining from sex for about a week every month, and hoping that the woman's "clock" would be nice and punctual. The efficacy of this method of contraception can be partially judged by large number of children in Catholic families.

It was inevitable that somebody would soon have to break ranks and shine some light on the difficulties faced by Catholics thinking of using the pill. A couple of British priests of the Catholic Church quite respectfully argued that the embargo on its use by the Church was creating great moral dilemmas for the faithful, and was forcing some to abandon their faith.

Letters, Catholic. It is heartening to Catholics to read in the press that at last members of religious bodies within the Church are speaking out against the archaic ruling on birth-control.

The latest "defector" states that he does not consider the church's teaching on birth-control as being in any way essential to Catholicism; this creates a ray of hope for those of us who find the practice of the "rhythm method" impracticable for many reasons, but are barred from receiving the Sacraments of Penance and Holy Communion. We cannot accept the ruling that the pill is against faith in God and Jesus.

The Church teaches that marriage is sacred and then proceeds to impose near impossible strains on couples who try to follow her teachings, causing heartbreak and unhappiness and making nervous wrecks of men and women over a facet of married life that should bring them joy and comfort.

It is this one ruling that causes more anguish than all the others put together, and is the reason for the large number of non-practising Catholics who, often because they are sincere, drift away from the practice of their religion and ultimately, most tragic of all, drift away from God altogether.

Letters, Tom Burton. I know that the Catholic Church places great value on tradition. I know too that it has had a tradition that will now make the pill illegal.

On the other hand, I can see that a most serious development in the world is that it is becoming over-populated, and that Africa and Asia are producing many more mouths than they can feed. Children born there are predestined to live in poverty all their lives, and suffer from famine and disease.

Surely, if it is the choice between this suffering on the one hand, and tradition on the other, the Church must decide to abandon its ban on the pill.

I have searched and searched both Testaments for anything that demands the banning of anything like the pill. I can find nothing. The Church's ban is based on an extra-Testament ruling by the Church itself, and should be supplanted by the very same Church.

Letters, Another Catholic. "Catholic" has unwittingly hit the nail on the head when she quotes Father Arnold McMahon as saying that the Catholic teaching on birth control is not an essential to Catholicism. The way the Church sees it, this teaching only clarifies the law of God which the Church cannot change.

At the same time the Church does not want to make married life harder than necessary and has been, and still is, encouraging research into ways of making the practice of the rhythm method easier. Catholics should ask a co-operative doctor about the latest developments or else write to the Catholic Welfare Bureau in their capital city.

I must add that the practice of the rhythm method is not easy and for some will always be harder than for others, but we were never led to expect that the Christian religion was easy and **with the help of prayer anything is possible**.

I would also like to point out that one of the basic principles of the Catholic Church is the infallibility of the Pope (not of the odd misguided priest) and those who decide they know better than the head of the Church in matters of faith and morals are Catholics in name only.

I have more reason than most for wishing to avoid further pregnancies but, for me as for millions of others, **what the Church says goes!**

Comment. This was the beginning of a controversy that has persisted to the present day. In 1962, the Catholic Church had initiated a series of discussions, called Vatican II, that brought together all the bishops of the Church in Rome to consider doctrinal issues. The whole on-and-off agenda took another three years to wrap up, so that you can see that haste was not an issue. Indeed, over the next decade and more, it seemed at times that Church's bishops might decide to change its ruling on contraceptives, but **after that it became clear that nothing would change**. That is, Catholics who use the pill were considered to be living in mortal sin, and were to be denied access to the Church's benefits.

This matter has continued to plague the Church, losing it numbers of practicing adherents, right up to the present.

RAPE AGAIN

In writing these books, I have found that rape keeps coming up as a major matter of public concern, year after year. There are lots of correspondents and judges and church people who have advocated stricter court sentences, castration, and whipping to stamp it out. In some States, until about ten years ago, there was a mandatory life sentence for adult rapists. Other people talked about treatment as for a psychological disease, others thought that the answer lay in the appreciation of religion.

Many other correspondents have theorised on the causes. The parents cop a lot of blame, or perhaps the schools, or the depravity in society generally. I can say with confidence that this is one of the few issues I have seen in covering these last 27 years where public opinion has advanced not at all.

So, I offer two Letters below. They don't provide much **practical** advice, but they deserve as much space as some of the other suggestions given over the years.

Letters, Sol Green. In Wednesday's "Herald" there was a letter "Brothels Counter To Rape." I fail to agree. **The cause of rape is over-feeding on inflammatory foods.** Personally I am not a vegetarian so-called. But three meals a day of blood meats and constipating white-flour breads, white sugar made from sugar cane, animal fats and so-called black puddings made of blood and white flour are the cause of rape.

Much of the trouble today re murder and rape, and uncontrolled anger, is caused by wrong feeding and a lack of knowledge of food values.

Letters, Only Human. I believe a lot of the blame for the sexual outrages occurring in such a spate recently must be placed at the doorstep of the moral reformers and the police who harass prostitutes and close down brothels.

It is impossible to legislate sexual desire out of man. All around us we see girls in bikinis showing themselves off; we see skirts past the knee, padded bosoms, low-cut frocks; we hear comedians telling blue jokes; we see films telling us that love in "Irma la Douce" style is fun.

When finally men succumb to all this suggestion and take direct action, rape may be the result, with a 10-year sentence in a grim prison. As I write this letter there are men within prison walls gripping the bars with despair, longing for their freedom. They are in for rape.

If brothels were open there would be no excuse for their actions. As I see it, a prostitute and her client make a deal to their mutual satisfaction; why should a third party step in? The police are egged on of course by the moralists.

Not everyone thought this was a proper policy to encourage.

Letters, Not So Silly. "Only Human," who advocates open prostitution, obviously does not realise the vast background of experience upon which the laws relating to the world's oldest profession are based.

It is not so very long ago when very young girls were recruited by money-hungry "madams," "pimps" and other very degraded human beings to satisfy the baser needs of corrupt and criminally selfish men and women. These unfortunate children, as indeed they were, were so young that they were in no position to decide for themselves whether they wished to "make a deal," as he so nicely puts it, with these poor unfortunate men who are unable to carry on without an adequate supply of sex.

During this same period older girls who were drawn into the vicious trap known as prostitution found it virtually impossible to escape from the tight security imposed by the people who ran the brothels. They were forced to pay for the rest of their useful "working" life for the mistake of allowing themselves to be led astray by unscrupulous people who made their living by recruiting girls for the brothels.

It was only after a long, hard battle, against the powerful brothel owners and the complete indifference on the part of the average citizen in such matters, that legislation was enacted to outlaw these practices.

Any move to repeal this legislation, or legislation passed since and based on it, would be so socially and morally backward that no thinking person could even entertain it.

STEP RIGHT UP, STEP RIGHT UP....

The Moscow Circus was again touring Australia. Most readers will remember circuses at that time, and one thing that everyone recalls is the animal acts. Elephants in the ring, sometimes on two legs, and sometimes on four. Walking in a daisy chain holding the tail of the beast in front. Spraying the audience with water from their trunks.

Then there were the lions and tigers, snarling and growling at their trainer as he made them sit up and perform. There was always the hope that one of them would break ranks, and eat the trainer, but his whip and voice saved him from that fate.

Of course, there were other acts. The trapeze artists flying high, and the jugglers, the strong man, the bearded lady, and the clowns. All jolly good fun, but overall, the animals were the best of all.

Letters, Frank Snow. Perhaps the current visit (just started in Melbourne) of the Moscow State Circus will serve to emphasise the steady decadence in recent years of, collectively speaking, the Australian circus. One only had to view a recent TV presentation of portion of the Russian show to realise this.

I don't for a moment suggest that local circuses were ever within reach even of aspiring to standards in Russia, where the circus, like the ballet, is by heritage and native culture part of that nation's whole character. In Russia today there are, I understand, no less than 7,000 persons wholly engaged in circus touring troupes and circus schools.

I'm not making that sort of comparison. What we should remember, however, is that the circus was once recognised as well and truly part of the Australian way of life, playing its own role and building its own tradition within the framework of our history. There was a time – and not so many years back, either – when such circus-family names as Wirth's, Bullen's, Sole's, Perry's and perhaps one or two others were really great in the land, names which sounded their own fascination in the realms of show business.

Most, perhaps all, such names are still on the circuit. But with nothing like the same following, and therefore with nothing like the same appeal. As a result, the standard of entertainment the Australian circus can offer these days is by economical necessity nothing like what it once was. This is but logical.

Less understandable is the apparent lack of concern about it. In a world of diverse leisure pursuits, of changing taste and shifting craze, Australia today is making an all-out effort to retain and promote some sort of public interest in the older and more basic sources of entertainment. We are succoring the theatre, shepherding the ballet and nursing the opera, even to the point of keeping a costly stream of Government-sponsored companies touring around the continent – and all more or less on public money. But not a thought for, not one penny-piece on, some effort to save the Australian circus!

In a country such as ours, which, for its environment and its virile people, might well be described as the circus's natural habitat, this sounds incredible. Perhaps the presence here of the stupendous Moscow Circus will help to put it in clear perspective.

Letters, A Eather. Your correspondent Frank Snow regrets the steady decadence in recent years of, collectively speaking, the "Australian circus."

To me there is one real and abiding tragedy – that of the performing animal. Once I believed all the silly, lying dope handed out to lazy-minded people concerning them. It is impossible to train animals for the ring by kindness!

When you participate in these spectacles you are paying to see the proceeds of cruelty – the final degradation of God's creatures.

Comment. This last Letter was one of the first stirrings of antagonism to the showing of trained animals in captivity. Since then, it has grown to the stage where, in Oz, the very wildest of circuses allow the petting of koala bears, though this too is generally forbidden .

You will all be aware that circuses by now have none of the great animal acts. Some of you will regret that. There are many arguments for and against this, but there is no doubt that circuses generally have lost their punch as a consequence.

APRIL NEWS ITEMS

Helena Rubenstein died on April 1ˢᵗ. She was the founder and developer of the **huge international beauty-products corporation** of that name. She was born in Poland in 1870, and **immigrated to Australia at the age of 32.** She developed her first beauty products from lanolin (from sheep), and pine bark lavender, and water lillies….

She was successful in selling her cosmetics in Britain, and moved to America in 1914, where she was in constant conflict with Elizabeth Arden. **She was the world's first female self-made millionaire.** Her height was 4 feet, 10 inches.

In NSW an interpretation of the **Laundry Employees' Award** is being enforced so that **self-service laundries will not be open at night, or after Saturday noon on weekends.** The Factories Act states that women cannot be employed during those hours. Most laundry attendants are women, so that will force the closure of the laundries….

Owners of laundromats intend to open next weekend and **will, if necessary, test the matter in the Courts.** A spokesman for the owners pointed out that in some overseas nations, including Britain and the US, some facilities were open 24 hours a day.

A Russian whaling fleet of 22 ships, (carrying 1,200 men) will berth in Sydney on April 8ᵗʰ. It has been operating off the coast of Western Australia for seven months. One of the vessels is a floating factory which cuts up the whales….

The Australian Minister for External Affairs has recently complained that **the fleet's operations were seriously affecting the Australian whaling industry**.

The Australian Parliament will make a gift of a 2,000 Pound milk bar to the Indian Parliament. It will serve milk drinks, soft drinks, and ice-cream. It was described by the manufacturer as the most glamorous, most elaborate milk bar ever to be exported from Australia.

A *SMH* report on April 10th reported that "fists and umbrellas flew" at a soccer match between NSW teams South Coast and Yugal. This is a reminder that **soccer was still a minor sport in Australia**, and that most followers of the sport were allied with European groups. It seemed that some of the **animosities from their homelands in Europe were being carried through into soccer in Australia**.

News item, April 18th. A 55-year-old man waiting for a bus was last night assaulted by four youths, and when he was on the ground, **they poured a bottle of methylated spirits over him and he was set alight.** His clothes caught fire and he was badly burned, and taken to hospital, where his condition is serious….

News item, April 19th. Another lad saw the attack, and spent today roaming the area with police. Late in the day, **he spotted the four miscreants, and they were arrested and charged.**

Thieves in the Sydney suburb of Cronulla have **stripped the lead from coloured glazed glass windows of several churches**. Police estimate that they would have needed a good-sized utility van to move all.

A trial shipment of **120 Corriedale sheep will leave Sydney this week for China.** This is despite the fact that **Australia's relationship with China is deteriorating daily** over mutual attacks in Indo-China.

More on soccer. Yesterday more than **100 Pan-Hellenic supporters** ran onto Wentworth Park and **attacked players and supporters of their opponent**, South Coast United.

A Perth correspondent lamented the fact that **marbles seems to have disappeared** from the activities of children.

BAG PIPES

For those of you who didn't make the last shower, bag pipes are so-called musical instruments played by Scotsmen who can't afford normal dress. The noise they emit is closer to the joyous screeches of mating cats than anything else, and they were often heard around New Years Eve, and Anzac Day, and any other procession or parade.

This correspondence was started by an anxious Letter from Kurrajong North, and then rolled on for weeks.

Letters, J McGuire. Could somebody explain why no radio stations broadcast any pipe music on New Year's Eve and New Year's Day? This lapse was an offence to all Celts, a number of whom in my hearing threatened to pack up and leave the country right then and there as we searched up and down the wavelength and found not one solitary skirl. Why? Why? Has the Sassenach stolen another march in the descent to Liverpool and Mersey and Mantovani?

Letters, Angele Gaebler. I cannot comment quickly, or strongly, enough on J McGuire's letter.

Why should other people endure it? Its excruciating howls are an offence and an abomination. If the Celts want that sort of thing let them all get together on the Domain – anywhere where no one else is put through such torture.

Where we spent our New Year's Eve, the management had the audacity to try and inflict it on us, but as one body we called the show off. No other nation has the consummate cheek to try and hog the scene in such a boorish and unseemly manner.

There are other nations – real nations, and not an isolated race in a suburb of England – with far more to give than just cat's music – but they have better manners.

Letters, Isabel Godfrey. Like J McGuire I deplore the absence of Scots music (bagpipes or otherwise) on radio and television on New Year's Day.

I wish to comment very strongly on the letter of Angele Gaebler. Scotland has no need to defend her proud record in song or story. The whole world knows of her glorious deeds in peace and war. Her bagpipe music has inspired men since time immemorial to fight and die for honour and the peace of the world. Her great men have given much to science and the arts.

A POST SCRIPT ON ANZAC DAY

You will remember a Letter in February that called for the termination of the Anzac Day marches after the last one this year. He had a bit of support at the time, though most writers to the *SMH* were against his proposal. Throughout March, Letters continued to flow in. They were almost all against the idea of cancelling Anzac Day as we knew it.

Now, with Anzac Day fast approaching, Letters picked up again, and I will publish two that seemed to summarise the dominant positions.

Letters, L P. Please don't let them debunk Anzac Day. A young man died in the rear turret of bomber over Italy in 1943. His name was Wally Lodge, of Adelaide. Every Anzac Day I buy two drinks and drink them both, one for Wally and one for myself.

I still see him with his dark hair and handsome face and beautiful teeth. That is how I remember him.

If the sourbellies want to spoil Anzac Day, let them play up the drink angle. In my squadron **the aircrew men always left a few pounds or guilders with the mess secretary to buy a round if they "bought it."** My money was spent once but I made it back.

Having a drink with an old friend is a pretty good tradition. Having one with a dead friend is good too. I'll bet that 22 years after my death no one will have a drink with me as I do with Wally.

Letters, Ralph Berman. Like other correspondents I too have neglected to march on Anzac Day. For the past decade I had found it too great an emotional strain. There were too many shadows marching with me, too many figures and faces that found a funeral pyre over Berlin or a mouldering grave in New Guinea. It even hurt too much to turn the wireless on, so that I deliberately closed my mind to Anzac and all that it means – or meant.

Recently I resolved however that no matter what the hurt I have a duty to my society to take part in this annual ritual. It was impressed upon me that there is a vast majority of our community to whom Anzac means nothing – those perhaps who escaped the experience or who benefited from the horror, or young people to whom the incident is but history, and ancient at that, or to whom "returned soldier" has come to be equated with poker machines, beer and anti-Communist witch-hunting.

People are forgetting. And when people forget they lose their defence. If the time ever comes when Anzac becomes meaningless, when war is forgotten and its horrors faded, then we will be due for another war.

ANOTHER ANZAC ISSUE

This year, Anzac fell on a Sunday. The programme for the march was the same as in previous years, right round Australia. That is, dawn services were due to be held in all major cities, and most towns. This would be followed by a march of veterans to some form of cenotaph, where a second service would be held. The parades would be over by about 11 o'clock, and then some of the veterans would meet up with old mates, and have a few beers and a good talk with these past comrades.

The trouble was, as I said above, that the Day fell on a Sunday. The Anglican Archbishop of Sydney indicated that because of this, he would not be attending the major service at the Sydney Cenotaph, because it was programmed to clash with the normal

Sunday service in his own Cathedral. Other Protestant clergy around the nation were confronted with the same situation, and also chose not to attend the public ceremonies that the diggers were ready to march to.

This was quite a dilemma. The Churches had held their own services for years at certain times on Sunday, and yet they were now expected to be somewhere else at the same time.

Tempers frayed, and the correspondence was voluminous.

Letters, G Richards. Two things should be said about the refusal of the State RSL to hold the Anzac Day March on Sunday afternoon, April 25, instead of Sunday morning, thus interfering with divine worship in many places.

First, why isn't the State president, Sir William Yeo, frank enough to enough to admit that a major reason why the league will not accede to the wishes of most Churches is that to have the march in the afternoon would mean that many of his members could not have an Anzac Day afternoon and evening free for drinking and gambling in the various RSL clubs? I know that such a statement will bring forth furious denials. But events on that day will prove that the RSL is anxious to get the march over in the morning and not interfere with the creature pleasures of its followers later in the day.

I write as an ex-Serviceman who places his morning devotions in God's house of worship **before** the claims of the RSL with its poker-machine, liquor-swilling philosophy.

Letters, T Clark. As a returned Serviceman of World War II, I wish to protest strongly against Dr Gough's decision not to participate in the Anzac Day Ceremony of Remembrance.

The next Anzac Day is of particular importance to those who wish it to be commemorated and there are many reasons why the march should be held in the morning. The Roman Catholic Church has seen fit to change the time for the main service, so why not others?

It seems to me that in these days of declining Church influence, the leaders of the Church should be concerned with bringing people back to the Church and not continually antagonising various sections of the community.

I will be present at the march to remember those who have passed on and to meet old friends again and will not be taking part in any "beer swill and gambling orgy" afterwards.

Letters, Hopeful Anglican. What a negative attitude the Anglican Church is taking in objecting to the Anzac March being held on a Sunday morning. The march itself is a solemn procession, culminating in a religious service, one of the few when people of different denominations can worship together. Surely the brotherhood of man is one of the ideals of our religion, and in the ceremonies of Anzac morning this feeling of brotherhood is predominant.

Instead of saying the march interferes with scheduled Church services, why not broadcast the Domain service to the suburban churches and invite the congregations to take part?

If the Anglican Church in Australia cannot make a change on a day like this, what hope has it of adapting itself to this rapidly changing world?

Letters, N Ongley. The march held on Anzac Day is, I believe, a part of a combined church parade – a march to a service to honour and remember all those who have made the supreme sacrifice.

Therefore, would it not have been the normal thing to do for the RSL authorities to make all arrangements in collaboration with all the Churches?

It would seem that in this State this is not so. The action of the RSL authorities does support the view expressed by G Richards that the RSL has its own activities in mind and is thus pledged to leave the afternoon free for other things.

Letters, (Mrs) F Smith. The Rev. Alan Walker says that a pagan is a man who places something else in the supreme place which can be occupied only by God, and he accuses the RSL of being pagan.

Anzac Day is primarily a commemoration of the sacrifice of men who died or suffered lifelong pain or injury. Sacrifice is surely the keynote of our Christian religion, and I would like to suggest that many of those whom we honour on Anzac Day found God, not in buildings of stone or in religious forms, but right there in the hearts of their fellow men. Anzac Day does not worship "State and traditions" as Mr Walker suggests, but the spirit of sacrifice. Is that paganism?

Letters, (Mrs) S P Oliver. I think the question of whether to march on Anzac Day or go to church boils down to one point. The fighting men themselves did not have time off to go to church when they had to fight, whether they wanted to or not.

God or the clergy did not stop the war on Sundays for the armies to attend church or have a day of rest. Sunday was as good a day for dying or fighting as any other day. There was no ban on killing on Sundays; work still went on on the Burma railway where my brother-in-law died; the Eighth Army kept fighting in the desert, where my brother was killed; Tobruk still held on and innocent people went to the gas chambers or starved in the concentration camps.

These men and innocent people had no choice; they were caught in circumstances from which God and the clergy could not extricate them. Because of them, however, we have got the choice of whether to march or not on a Sunday morning. They died on Sundays whether it was during church service time or not, so I think it is up to us to remember them and march with their comrades and, while we are doing it, to be thankful that they have given us the freedom of choice.

Comment. Twenty-odd years earlier during WWII, and before, the churches were very powerful institutions in the community. For example, when they called for **days of prayer** for peace and the welfare of particular invaded countries and the like, church attendance soared and supplicants were many. Since then however, the influence of the churches had waned. Right now, for example, in the middle of the 1965 nation-wide drought, the many calls for a national day of prayer were met with many grunts of contempt at the very thought. The churches had lost some of their punch.

Yet, the controversy over the services on Anzac Day makes the point that they were by no means a spent force. When confronted by a powerful body advocating a different timetable for services, they were **able to split the community about fifty-fifty.** So that on the day in question, the attendances at the various marches and services were up to expectations, but attendances at the churches were bigger than normal. The Churches had lost some of their punch, but were not yet flat on their backs.

Comment 2. Would this year's march be the last? Clearly not. Fifty years later, in the year 2015, there were huge turnouts. because of the 100th anniversary of Anzac. But for the previous decade, attendances have grown and grown, and it seemed that the younger generations were becoming more appreciative of the nation's military heritage. **So, will Anzac Day go away? In my opinion, not very likely.**

THE MAVIS BRAMSTON SHOW

Australia got TV in 1956. By 1965, it had the ABC, and the Seven and Nine networks, and Ten was just starting up. Most of our drama and entertainment came from the US, with live shows like the Andy Williams and the Perry Como Shows dominating. The Brits did their bit in the world of satire, with *This Was the Week that Was* and *Not Only but Also....* getting a good following.

Late in 1964, Channel Seven produced a new, Australian **satire** show that featured Gordon Chater, Noeline Brown, Barry Creighton, and June Salter as permanents, and dozens of other Oz and overseas celebrities. In the familiar format of the overseas shows, it had a number of skits, and a few singers, and occasional brass bands and marching troupes. For Oz audiences, it was a grand spectacle every week, and the show was very popular.

It stood out from the overseas shows, however, because it was not a goody-goody show like the Americans produced, and the satire was more biting than the not-so-mild British. Also, it was full of school-boy smut, sexual double entendres, and lecherous insinuations. Australians had been relatively starved of such fare, and were ready to sit back and smirk as the monotonous so-called humour was repeated week after week. Eventually, after three years the show had reached its use-by-date, and it folded.

The following Letters capture some of the more critical feelings that emerged near the end of the first season.

Letters, (Mrs) Ruth Lewis. When I viewed the first edition of the current TV program, "The Mavis Bramston Show," I wanted to write the first fan letter of my life. This program was like a breath of fresh air to the stale local scene and gave promise of being a rival to "The Week That Was" of overseas fame.

After viewing Wednesday night's edition of the same show how thankful I am I didn't write that fan letter. The emphasis was on smut. We were treated to skits on illegitimate babies and "The Pill" and even flower arrangements were the subject of smutty sexual "jokes."

What puzzles me most is why the cast, for the most part talented, lend themselves to such second-rate material. Even Ruth Cracknell, a comedienne in her own right, has to descend to the accepted low level. Farewell "Mavis Bramston."

Letters, Grant C Roberts. I have viewed on a number of occasions the current "Mavis Bramston" show on Channel 7. Considering that this is a television show and, in addition, on a national network, I have always been surprised at the number of risqué remarks and "sketches" contained in each show.

Wednesday night's show provided more of these acts on a still lower level. I refer particularly to the "sketch" about floral arrangements. This, in my opinion, should never have been allowed on a TV show. The producers could not blame the viewers' dirty minds, as, in this case, they left no alternative.

It seems that these people intend to get away in this regard with a bit more every week and that their sponsors and those who are responsible for censoring TV programs are turning the blind eye to it. It's a pity that talented artists have to resort to this form of humour to get a laugh.

No doubt I'll be branded as a "square" for daring to question the morals of such a show, but if all the other programs accept the standard that has been set and follow suit, heaven help the future generation.

Comment. This last Letter says a lot. It was a show that promoted juvenile smut, and the more publicity it got, the smuttier it became. The more publicity it got through the outraged cries of the professionals and the genuinely affronted parents, the faster the viewing audience grew.

There were sensible arguments put forward that said it was fulfilling a function of mocking a number of sacred cows. I remember thinking at the time that was true, and worthwhile. But it was obvious to me that there weren't so many such cows available, and it would quickly run out of chaff. That is what happened to it, and the producers switched instead to the smut that would always have a longer-life market. By the time Mavis died, there were few mourners.

BALL-POINT PENS

Letters, James Gardner. If education is meant to be a preparation for life, why are primary school children not allowed to use ball-point pens, and are forced instead to use old-fashioned steel pens and nibs. The only place where these things are used today is the Lottery Office.

Letters, Olive Short. Lottery offices are definitely not the only places where steel nibs are used. As an accountant I use one, as does the assistant secretary of our company. I would not think of writing in a ledger with a ballpoint. They have taken all character out of handwriting and thank goodness the Education Department is sensible enough to see that children maintain some individuality in their writing. Anyone can scribble with a ballpoint.

Letters, T Murphy. I am a primary school teacher with thirty years experience. I have taught thousands of children to write. It is very difficult for them, and they all hate the experience. The pens they have are all old, the ink is a constant menace, and many of them do not have the manipulative skills to do a proper job. So writing lessons are a horror.

The powers that be want everyone to write in copperplate, and even provide templates for the children to practice into. This is ridiculous, since all of them are not physically mature enough. To say that certain strokes should be thin, and others should be thick, only shows how thick these people are.

The aim of writing is to communicate and to do business. If we can devise better ways of doing this, we should grab them and use them all the time. Give me and my children a biro every time. If anyone wants to write like a calligrapher, they should do a course on it – when they are adults.

Comments. These Letters take me back to my primary school days, and what a frightful mess it always was struggling with pen and ink, and inkwells, and blotting paper, and ink on your fingers, and clearing up spills. Where did those small hairs come from that clogged up the nibs?

One device that the above writers did not mention was the **fountain pen**. For me, this came **after** pen and ink, and **before** ball-points. This could also be messy when being filled, but was pretty good. Then came **the bliss of ball-points**. Recall your first BIC? Mine, at least, was heaven. Though **refills** were sometimes hard to get.

MAY NEWS ITEMS

Legalised phone betting on the TAB will start in NSW at the end of May.

Confronted with the growing **high-society fashion of the kissing of ladies' hands,** Roger Semet, a French author, threw in his bit of nonsense. "I'm all in favour of hand-kissing. After all, one must start somewhere."

Sydney University students claimed a world record when they **crammed 94 students into a borrowed hearse.**

The book **"Let's Stalk Strine"** by Professor Afferback Lauder **was released in Australia.** It was an analysis of the Australian language. The Lauder name was a pen name used by a local graphic artist, Alistair Ardoch Morrison….

The book took the mickey out of our way of talking. The first copy of the book was given to **the retiring Governor General, Lord de L'Isle**, at Mascot Airport as he was leaving at the end of his appointment here….

Remember "Emma chisit?' "Egg nishner", "egg wetter gree"?

The age of innocence. A front-page Press report of the trial of a woman before the court told how she had bought a small packet of marijuana from a man in a café in Sydney's Rose Bay. She said "I did not realise how serious it was when I bought the drugs." My, how things can change.

The NSW Cricket Association has decided to give payments to **retired** players who played for NSW, and who played **30 or more Tests for Australia. They will receive 25 Pounds for each Test.** Three players are currently eligible. Keith Miller, Arthur Morris, and Ray Lindwall….

Richie Benaud and Alan Davidson did not now qualify because they have not yet retired....

Keep in mind that all players were amateurs in those days. This was the only payment they got. Contrast that with 50 years later when some of the stars earn a million dollars a year from the game. Again, how things can change.

A 19-year-old sailor and his Melbourne fiancé were disappointed yesterday. He is in Melbourne for a week with an American fleet. The couple met, and within days decided to marry. He got permission for his Commanding Officer, and they went to the Melbourne Registry Office....

They were told that under the **new Commonwealth law, couples must apply for a licence to marry, and then wait a week before the marriage can take place**. He has only a few days before his fleet sails. The seven-day rule can be shortened in certain circumstances, but in this case, the shortening was not approved. **They were photographed by the *SMH*, outside the registry office, looking gloomy. The couple were not able to marry, in fact. Ever. When he went home with the fleet, they both lost interest.**

The World Heavyweight Title fight between **Cassius Clay and Sonny Liston** will be the first such fight to **be carried live across the Atlantic** by the new Early Bird satellite.

Don Athaldo, world-renowned strongman, died at home in **the NSW town of Ettalong**. He appeared in competitions and circuses for fifty years, and held **486 medals for his feats of strength**. His death was discovered when he did not go to a near-by farm to get his daily goat-milk.

A 47-year-old man, Bill Harper, says he is **the last rabbit-o in Sydney**. He has a 19-year-old horse, Dolly, and together they will try to be the first to use the new large Taren Point Bridge near Sydney when it opens on Monday. He says that the law gives precedence to horse-drawn vehicles.

THE VIETNAM WAR IS STILL BUILDING

To let you know that the **Vietnam and South East Asia disturbance is still ongoing**, I include a few headlines and items, and these were all taken randomly from the first few weeks in May. I suggest you do not worry about the detail, but use them to keep in the back of your mind that **this conflict, US (and others) versus the Reds,** was gradually getting more serious.

Arrival of the First Royal Australian Battalion in Vietnam is expected today.

President Johnston has announced that all **Vietnam** and its surrounding waters **is now classified a combat zone**.

US jets attacked trains and railways in North Vietnam today, but the attacks were moderated because of the danger of civilian casualties on May Day.

The Australian Minister for External Affairs said that the trouble in Asia posed "**a World War threat**." "South-East Asia is in the front line in the struggle for world security."

Headlines: US paratroops for South Vietnam in a few days.

Students, waterside workers and Quakers were among the crowds that **demonstrated against the sending of Australian troops to Vietnam today.**

Headlines: Mass attack by Vietcong. Seven Americans killed.

In Vietnam, 26 US military were killed when **10 planes, fuelled and loaded with bombs, blew up on the runway at one of their bases**. At least 70 more were injured, and 12 other planes were destroyed. It is reported that **this was an accident**, and not the work of Vietcong guerrillas.

Russia says Australia is aggressor: our troops in Vietnam.

A UNIVERSITY FOR NEW GUINEA

Australia had a mandate from the United Nations to run the affairs of Papua New Guinea. Part of this mandate was to lift the standard of **education** in the Territory. In the 20 years since WWII, much effort had been put into this, and a primary school system had been set up in the more accessible regions, and also secondary education was available in the more populated areas.

In 1965, the first PNG native graduated at a university (Sydney). This raised a number of suggestions that it was timely to establish a university there. Mr Manning, a resident of PNG, commented on this.

He pointed out that he had an Honours degree from Sydney University, and had taught in Sydney High schools. He was now teaching in PNG, and was of the opinion that it was not yet timely to start a university in the Territory. He argued thus:

Letters, P W Manning, Konedobu, Papua. First, the education system here is not adequate. I do not say that the Education Department is not trying or that things are not slowly improving. However, I deal with a number of indigenes daily, mostly claiming Standard 6-8, which is supposed to be equivalent to first to third year secondary school. The fact is that most of my lads are at mid-primary in a few subjects and untouched in the rest. I have taught at Sydney High schools, and I am sure of this. The indigenes are not unintelligent, mark you; they are uneducated.

Then he went on to the cost. He said that under a reasonable set of assumptions, the cost to produce a graduate would be 20,000 Pounds, and that was prohibitive. He went on to argue that their secondary schools could not provide enough students to build classes big enough for universities.

What he wanted instead was an institution that would provide badly-needed technicians, and another to provide agricultural training. He concluded that for the "next 20 years, let us send deserving students to Australia, where they can gain a worthwhile degree at far smaller cost."

Comment. Under the United Nation's mandate, inspectors were sent out every three years to check on how well we were doing in bringing the joys of civilisation to the natives. These inspectors were most often ideologically driven, and always found we were doing well, but could do better in many things. Education was one matter which they harped on, and one that we were particularly interested in.

So in 1965, with a visit fast approaching, the University of Papua New Guinea was established, despite the arguments of Mr Manning. It now (2019) has five campuses and 13 study centres, and a student body of 16,000.

HOW ABOUT ROO SHOOTING? GERMANS?

What was the public's attitude to shooting roos? After all, a case could be made out that they were of great nuisance to farmers, and their numbers in most outback areas were creating havoc with fences and pastures. An American woman, Mrs Robert Grimm, renowned in the US as a hunter, had tired of killing elephants and tigers and the like, and wanted a spot of sport killing off our faster-moving kangaroos.

She was quoted in the Press as saying "I have hunted almost every animal, including tigers with the King of Nepal, mountain sheep with the Shah of Iran, and red deer with General Franco of Spain."

The gentleman below was not impressed.

Letters, Theo Bogue Atkinson, President, Protection of Animals, Sydney. I refer to a news paragraph in the

"Herald" about an American woman, Mrs Robert Grimm, coming here to shoot kangaroos. It is intensely distasteful to me personally, and I am sure to very many others, that people from other countries should come here to indulge their killing instincts, and blaze away at our wildlife.

The fact that this woman is a mother of four children makes one wonder just where the tide of compassion rises and falls in the human make-up, and especially so when the possibility of killing a mother kangaroo with its baby in its pouch comes to mind. In any case, we are under the impression that to kill kangaroos it is necessary now to possess a current licence. What authority would grant this to a stranger to our shores?

Comment. Just one more sign of society's emerging urge to protect animals.

Letters, German Migrant. I am a German migrant and have been in Australia some eight years. During the last war I was in the German Army, but I was not a Nazi.

I love your country, which is now my home, but I do not like seeing and do not like my children seeing war films on TV like "12 O'Clock High," "Combat," etc. It is bad for the children and a bad thing for German migrants. We all like working here and we like our work-mates, but we do hate getting all hell knocked out of us on TV a few times a week.

Please can't these pictures be stopped or are they to drag on for ever?

Letters, A Fenton. In reply to "German Migrant" I would suggest that if he does not like seeing "all hell knocked out of us," on the programs he sees, to switch to one of the other two channels.

Does he seriously expect to see the reverse happening on a war series made in an Allied country? What would he expect to see on a film made by a German company?

As for declaring that he was in the German Army but not a Nazi, this always makes me smile. I have met and known many Germans both here and in England, but not one ever admitted he was a Nazi. I am forced to the conclusion, therefore, that the only Nazi in Germany was Adolf Hitler.

MERCY KILLING

A 67-year-old Sydney man was sentenced to two year's prison for the manslaughter of his wife. She had been in pain for years, and had earlier tried to kill herself by fire. Her medical condition was hopeless, and the killing was done with full co-operation of the deceased. In effect, **it was the classic mercy killing.**

The judge at the trial said that the man was a "very decent man" and appeared to be close to tears as he made his judgement. However, he intoned that the community would not tolerate mercy killing.

A number of prominent people commented. Professor Stout, from the Department of Philosophy at Sydney University, said that "hopelessly ill people in pain should be entitled to commit suicide **with the approval of a suitable tribunal.**" His, however, **was a lone voice.**

Protestant and Catholic spokesmen condemned all forms of euthanasia. The Director of the Catholic Information Bureau said "I would not hesitate to condemn the action as immoral. To God alone it belongs to give life or take it away. No human being can take the responsibility into his own hands".

The principal of the Anglican Moore Theological College backed him up. "We have not got the right to terminate our own lives, or the lives of others. This is because God is the author of life, and He has not delegated to us the right to take it."

The Secretary of the AMA said the medical profession was unable on ethical grounds to support the idea of euthanasia. "Its position has never varied. Doctors are pledged to save and maintain life"

Comment. You can see that the major institutions were firmly set against euthanasia. Nor was there much support for it from the community. Only one Letter was printed by the *SMH* on the matter.

Letters, Anne Howard Toes. The suggestion of Professor Stout, as reported in Saturday's "Herald", that, "while individual persons should not have the right to carry out euthanasia, hopelessly ill persons should be entitled to commit suicide 'with help' if this were approved by a suitable tribunal," is a much needed solution to a very grave problem. Such a tribunal would, of course, be necessary to ensure that a "mercy" killing should not be used as a cloak for murder.

What I cannot understand is the Churches' attitude in this matter. What rational explanation has any Church for its insistence on certain commandments or parts of commandments being obeyed literally, while allowing latitude with others. Some are impossible. How could we keep the commandment enjoining "no manner of work" on Sundays for instance? Christ himself set the example for breaking that one. So why should the Churches deplore "mercy killings" when it countenances killing in war and killing as a punishment for crime?

The conclusion from all this is that mercy killing was not very much of the public agenda. Indeed, here we are **fifty years later**, and still it is still in the too-hard basket for politicians to take a firm stand on. Too many votes could be lost because the churches stand resolutely against it.

Yet I wonder: Would all or some of the church-going population vote (in 2019 in favour of euthanasia even though their own Church opposed it? At the moment, such a vote is getting closer by the day.

THE TEEMING TEENS

The **baby boom** started rather limply in 1946. By 1965, it has just about run its course. But by that time, the fruits of much endeavour had grown, so that teenagers were hitting the headlines. There were now more teenagers on the prowl **than ever before**, and the number was growing. This was good for marketing types, retailers and the like, because they also had more money and more freedom **than ever before**. The prosperity, and the freedom from many restrictions that narked previous generations, created a great liberating experience for the youngsters, and indeed, for all society, and despite all the nostalgia for the olden times, was a pretty good thing.

Some of these teenagers however, were causing problems. This was nothing new, but it seemed that the number of annoying breaches was increasing too fast for comfort. The newspapers were full of examples of crass behaviour. **Letters** condemned the hordes of teenagers crowding into trains, shouting from one end of the carriage to the other end. They blocked the aisles, stood in the doorways, jostled the elderly, spat at people on the platforms. They had fights, they swore, they vomited, they drank alcohol, they piddled out the doors.

Beyond that, however, there were more serious considerations. The number of serious teenage crimes was on the increase, including the occasional murder. More obviously, teenage drinking was on the increase.

News item. Up on the stage a shapely brunette opened her mouth and began belting out a song. Down on the floor, watching her, about 300 happy teenagers opened their mouths – and began putting away beer in large quantities.

Outside the afternoon shone. But the boys and girls in this Sydney suburban hotel were finding their fun indoors, listening to a pop group. And drinking, drinking, drinking....

For the young people of this city have well-developed thirsts. And they are quenching them in a manner which would horrify parents.

The legal age for drinking in New South wales is 18. But I find disturbing the numbers of young people under this age – or who have barely reached it – who have already assumed the air of bar-room veterans.

Part of the reason for this is that many hotels are no longer just places where one goes only for a drink. The pop group now seems to be as much a part of many pubs as the beer keg. All over the city groups of amiable young men strum guitars, beat drums, twist and shout and make their fans squeal with delight.

These are the type of performers recently described by an eminent Sydney headmistress as being able to convert young people into a "hypnotised mob of unstable passions."

Be that as it may, they are also the type of performers the teenagers want. Theirs is the sound that excites. To listen to it – and sometimes dance to it – the kids are following the pop boys into the pubs. Once there they do not for long stick to lemonade.

Comment. Of course, this has become the norm over the past 50 years. At the time, though, **it was all very new**. The idea that teens could find an exclusive venue, drink beer, and dance and gyrate, was something their parents would never have thought of.

Not everyone thought it was a good thing. This writer puts his perspective on it.

Letters, W Maguire. There is ample evidence of this emerging pattern of social behaviour after 10 years of 10 p.m. closing in NSW. As a member of the NSW Temperance Alliance, and one who is actively engaged in youth welfare work through my own church affiliation, I find that, with all the talk of increased facilities and further outlets for the supply of alcoholic beverages, there has been a marked increase in juvenile drinking.

The Licensing Bench of NSW, in its annual report for the year ended December, 1963, confirmed this situation when it said: "The feature which gave cause for the most concern during the year was the large number of prosecutions which came before the Court alleging the presence of persons under 18 years in the bars of hotels and the supply of liquor to such person .... no doubt 10 o'clock closing and entertainment have contributed to the presence in hotels of these young persons, but some licensees have provided 'stomp' music and similar types of entertainment and it is almost inevitable in these circumstances that persons under age will be attracted to their hotels."

Just recently a Crown prosecutor said that the increased number of juveniles drinking in hotels was becoming "a serious problem." So, with all those wiseacres who argued that 10 p.m. closing would end the 6 o'clock "swill" and usher in "civilised" drinking, we now face a more serious social and moral problem which is emerging as a direct consequence of wide-open hotel trading well into the evening. Our legislators can be held responsible for ever increasing the scope for the consumption of alcoholic liquor without due regard to the moral and social consequences.

Another writer had an interesting suggestion to save something from the mayhem.

Letters, (Mrs) Y E Rentoul. Your recent article brings to attention an even more vital need, a form of compulsory savings for teenagers. In these days of high wages the spending capacity of young people is quite fantastic. Most of their money is dissipated on entertainment, extensive and extravagant wardrobes and unnecessary cars. Yet, when the time comes for marriage there is little, if anything, saved and we are constantly being ear-bashed about how impossible it is for young married couples to acquire their own homes. If the money wasted by both parties in their early earning days had been saved, a deposit on a home would be readily available on marriage.

Under a compulsory savings scheme, money could be drawn off at the source in the same way as PAYE taxation. This money would then be held in trust for each individual in an interest-earning savings account, and the money would be withdrawable on marriage or for setting up in business or in trade. There can certainly be no moral objection to such a plan on the grounds that it interferes with the right of the individual. The system operated throughout the war years for all members of the Armed Services in the form of deferred pay without accruing interest. How much more justifiable would such a system be in our present economy?

Comments. There was a great deal more to be said on teen behaviours, and indeed it filled many columns of print over the ensuing years. Much of it had a moralistic flavour, with the implication that these rampant youths were not quite what we wanted, and **they might come to a sticky end**. This was especially so with the introduction of drugs onto the scene a few years later. Yet, the teens were becoming such a big market, they were hard for the papers to criticise too much.

In any case, many of these young tear-aways are now the readers of my books. I think I will leave it to you to decide if indeed your end was all that bad.

SOCIETY RECOGNISES A NEW GROUP

On May 14th, the *SMH* carried a letter from a writer who informed readers that a new society was being formed in Adelaide to benefit a number of children who had recently been **diagnosed as autistic**. This malady, only recently recognised as being distinct from schizophrenia, caused "severe emotional disturbances or mental illnesses" and required attention that was quite distinct from any previous method attempted.

He appealed to parents in other States to contact him, so that some form of national association could be formed to better serve the sufferers.

This was apparently the beginning of the formation of a society that is well known across Australia today.

JUNE NEWS ITEMS

Lithgow in NSW has an unanswered mystery. **Do you remember matches**, those things you used to light fires with? Those small sticks of wood, fifty to a box, one-and-a-half inches long with a red phosphorous–type head that you would rub against an abrasive on the box?....

These boxes of matches, bundled into packets of 16, **were suddenly exploding in Lithgow**. For no apparent reason. Eight such packets had recently exploded. The manufacturer has no explanation, and it is not happening elsewhere.

Comment. This mystery was never solved, despite much comment and effort.

Many **legal professionals** and some Bar Associations were agitating to **remove juries** from deciding how much compensation should be paid **for accidents and workers compensation....**

The argument **for** this was that **juries were granting larger-than-needed sums** out of sympathy for the injured. The argument **against** it was that **judges were out of touch with real-life costs and would grant smaller-than-needed sums**. The argument was settled over time with the jury system largely removed in most States.

Two large trade deals with Japan were done by mining company R W Miller (also a brewer). This was the beginning of a new way of trading with Japan, and another step in the process of forgiving, if not forgetting, WWII. **On both sides.**

Some official in the US, leading something called **the Apollo Space Program,** said the US could put **men on the moon before the year 1970. Comment.** I can tell you with certainty that this is **typical American wild talk. It will never happen. Absolute rubbish.**

Customs officers and police are worried that **the taking of narcotic drugs is on the increase**. While not a problem at the moment, they say they are aware of the situation in America, and **do not want Australia to go down the same path**. The drug of choice here is **still marijuana, though heroin is on the increase.**

In the Queen's Birthday Honours list, the four Beatles were each given an OBE.

When **the South African Rugby Union team** arrived in Melbourne, it was met by demonstrators who complained that **the team had no black players**. "None of sufficient quality", said the manager. The demo was part of **a bigger protest against apartheid generally**.

A survey by the Woolgrowers and Graziers Council said that **one third of Australia is now affected by drought**. This could become the **worst drought in Australia's history**.

Five members of a railway fettlers gang were killed near Gladstone, Queensland, when a 1,000-ton coal train hit their **motorised trolley**.

American actress Jane Powell was married in Sydney today. The ceremony was attended by 27 guests and 2,000 "gawkers." Also present were Powell's three children. It was her third marriage.

Australian 20-year-old youths were being conscripted to do National Service. At present those selected, on the basis of drawing their birthdays from a barrel, were having **medical examinations.** So far, 29 per cent have failed this....

Out of 41,000 lads drawn out of the barrel, 133 had registered as **conscientious objectors.** They will be required to serve in a non-military capacity. That is, **do dogs-body work** about the camps, and be **subjected of ridicule** by some other recruits.

ALPHABET SOUP

Many of you will remember alphabet soup. It was sold in little meal-sized packets that contained dried ingredients for soup, and a random collection of pasta-pieces made into the letters of the alphabet. The idea was to make the soup, and then float the characters on top, and this whirling, cavorting universe of letters would make a diverting meal for children and the like. It all seemed harmless enough.

Grave moral danger lurked, however.

Letters, W Caukill. The other day my family and I were sitting down to dinner, eating our first course, which consisted of a certain proprietary vegetable soup in which the manufacturers include letters of the alphabet made from noodles.

Imagine my horror when I saw, floating on the surface of the soup being eaten by my eight-year-old son, one of the **four-letter words** used by that dreadful man D H Lawrence.

When will the Government do something to prevent this disgraceful situation by banning the use of letters which form these disgusting words?

Comment. For some reason, this report of the corruption of young minds made me laugh. Quickly, though, I saw the seriousness of the situation, and started to wonder whether the writer was serious, or whether he was simply a depraved person out for a leg-pull.

As it turned out, though, a couple of writers confirmed my worst fears, told me how serious the situation was, and let fly with a well-earned admonition of Mr Caukill.

Letters (Mrs) G Clarke-Cottrell. I find it difficult to believe that anyone intelligent enough to form coherent sentences either in speaking or writing should commit themselves in print to such ridiculous statements. The odds are fantastic against noodles floating in a bowl of soup accidentally forming a word – good or bad – without any assistance.

The suggestions that certain letters be left out of the noodle alphabet in a packet of soup would be funny were it not so frightening. We may as well omit those offensive letters from the alphabet which the children learn at school – or from the alphabet blocks with which they play in kindergarten.

Personally I find books larded with crudities rather boring reading and, therefore, do not go out of my way to read them. But to search one's soup bowl for dirty words seems to me to indicate a funny sort of mind. I shudder to think of the psychological mess any child would grow into if exposed to such self-righteousness for long. For the sake of sanity, do realise that such ridiculous censorship can only drive youngsters into the most unpleasant paths of exploration. Apart from anything else, surely the Government can find something more important to do than concern itself over soup noodles. Has Mr Caukill considered how small the alphabet would be if we were to delete every letter that could possibly be used to spell a dirty word?

Letters, A Prior, Bankstown. In reply to the rather foolish Caukill letter, I should like to ask whether the reader expects the alphabet to be changed to exclude all letters which form offensive words. Absolute rot! Most eight-year-olds would not understand the meaning of these words, unless horror was shown. Soup in my house is made to be eaten, not read.

There was more to come, however. This little Letter below turned me again towards the idea that the original Letter was indeed a leg-pull.

Letters, P J Marshall, Balgowlah. Regarding a letter headed "Chatterley Soup" which you published on Thursday concerning that dreadful alphabet soup – I haven't had such a good laugh for ages!

Then the matter was put beyond doubt. Mr Caukill came back with a long Letter, in which he **firstly** admitted that his original letter was fictitious and ridiculous. He decried those respondents whom he considered to have lost their capacity for logical and constructive thought. He went on to say that their efforts were "the stuff of which bigots are made, and from which intolerance and persecution arise."

Secondly, he went on to make an **interesting argument about censorship**. He saw the soup example as similar to the efforts of governments and moralists to remove some books, plays and painting from the public reach. He argued that every would-be censor had their own selection of arty-things that offended him. If they were free to remove these, like letters from a soup, they would, one after another, remove everything until, so to speak, there was nothing left in the soup.

He argued that all the letters should be left floating for his children. If some of them offended, or gave off a wrong message, it was not up the censors to impose blanket bans on them, but (in his case) it was the parent's responsibility to remove, or discuss and explain, the offensive letters.

He concluded with the suggestion that "Finally, we should be teaching our children to strive for the rights of others to disagree with them. If we are successful, censorship and other interferences with the rights of the individual, will become superfluous."

Comment. Now that Mr Caukill has led me cleverly into making comment on censorship, I must admit I have no simple rules. On the one hand, in theory, I am against all forms of censorship. But when I am confronted with some of the excesses of vulgarity, violence, and degradation that are purveyed in our society, I am deeply offended, and say there is no place for them.

I think I am no different from many other people. Back in 1965, I think that many of the "governments and moralists" were too severe. So I welcome the relaxation that has undoubtedly occurred. But do I think it has gone too far? Certainly not. **Except when it offends me. Then I want to take a few letters off the soup.**

SCHOOL PROJECTS

The 1960's was the decade of **the school project**. It seemed that every kid in school, from the youngest to the oldest, had a project every term where they had to get some knowledge, put it in a folder, and pretty it up with pictures and drawings.

For example, one such project might have been to examine steel-making in Australia. One place to start was in the school library, but as the years passed, competition in these matters got stiffer, and so there was a need to get material from closer to the source. So, adventurous families wrote to suppliers of this and that, and asked for descriptive material of any of the processes involved in production. BHP, the maker of most of our steel, was a popular target, and it had reams of literature specially printed to satisfy the multiple enquiries for good-looking inserts for the school projects.

Companies, big and small, were all expected to have hand-outs ready for school kids. Some of these companies found the whole system very trying.

> **Letters, Arthur Neve.** I am the proprietor of a business, and, possibly because I am getting old and crotchety, the attitude of the scores of children who write to us for help in their "projects" is rather getting me down!
>
> I am quite willing to help, but.... Teachers in an increasing number of schools are setting holiday "projects" dealing with solar energy and, individually, girls and boys write or telephone us asking for illustrated information. As soon as we send to one, the grapevine gets to work, and other requests pour in.
>
> Each time we write, printed matter and postage (not to mention time) cost us about 2/6. No one ever sends postage and no one ever acknowledges or thanks us for what we send them.
>
> I am sure that other firms similarly approached would much prefer to send this information in bulk to the teacher concerned prior to the work being set. If sent to individual

children, as at present, an occasional word of thanks from the recipient would ensure that future requests were attended to.

Letters, Parent, Lane Cove. Arthur Neve brought up an aspect of school projects that has become almost a public nuisance – that is soliciting information from commercial firms.

It has been my experience, as the mother of two school-children, that the main requirement for these projects is pictures of the subject. To get these, the pupils are encouraged to cut up publications of any sort, some costing the parents quite a lot (often two copies of each are required), others from institutions and firms such as Mr Neve's at an expense of time and money to them.

Most children these days are within reasonable distance of good municipal libraries where all this information can be found. Admittedly they have to copy diagrams and pictures, but it is my opinion that they learn far more while doing this, not only about their subjects, but about research from books in general, than they ever would from cutting up pamphlets.

My 12-year-old daughter recently spent weeks doing a project which she illustrated by meticulous drawings, all copied from library textbooks, but was penalised for not having enough "pictures." Are these projects designed for education or for presenting a pretty picture book to parents at displays of work?

Letters, George Graham. Recently I was asked to inspect a dozen school projects done on coal mining. I was greatly discomforted and annoyed by what I saw.

To be brief, the material presented looked like it had been prepared for Hollywood. It had all the glamour pictures you could imagine, lots of happy miners, long train loads of coal, happy miners' wives, and the wonderful grounds of the local Mine Rescue Station.

It had nothing to do with coal mines as I know them. The incredibly hard work, the falls of coal, the injuries, the deaths at the coal-face, the stoping, the dust and the spitting of blood. The brattice, the pillars, the drives and shafts, the ponies, the 24-ton dargs, the wheelers. I could go on.

Then I looked at how they were marked. The flashier ones got a good mark. The prettier, the better. Anyone who tried to come to grips with the content of mining was badly marked down.

School projects like these are a sham.

Comment. The concept of the school project lingers on in 2019, though not nearly so prevalent as it was. Now, however, no one has to scrounge round from commercial firms, and can instead get all the needed material via the internet.

SCOUTING AND GIRL GUIDES

Letters, Householder. While in no way wishing to detract from the merits of the Freedom from Hunger Appeal, has not the time come for a compulsory halt to be called to these Sunday doorknock appeals?

One has become accustomed to the mail being flooded with art union tickets one did not order or want, the Friday street appeals, the incessant telephone appeals which disrupt the business community, and the repeated visits from mendicants of various associations and religious orders. One may even become adjusted to the personal delivery of ball tickets by our "understaffed" uniformed police, with all the implied dangers of non-donation.

One will, however, refuse to become accustomed or adjusted to the repeated invasion of private homes on the Sabbath. There should be once and for always, a central community chest for the distribution and collection of donated moneys.

Comment. One form of door-knock that was very popular was the Bob-A-Job venture for scouts, and a similar one called Willing Shilling for guides. Both saw young people go out into the community, once or twice a year, and go from house to house offering to do small jobs for the payment of a minute fee. It was a neat way of fundraising, and was also seen as a good way to give these youngsters some valuable life experiences.

A correspondent, called BE PREPARED, wrote a lengthy Letter, in which he was critical of the schemes. Referring specifically to the Scout's efforts, he said that their records showed that they got money for absolute trivia. He saw entries for emptying a tea-pot, bringing in the milk bottle, hosing the patio, and setting the table. Each of these got one shilling.

He writes "This is absurd, and gives children a ridiculous idea of the value of money, and what they themselves expect to be paid in the commercial world."

In his own case, he set the children to hosing the garden. Within a few minutes, "they were lined up watching some horses. I paid them six shillings, and sent them on their way. It wasn't worth it."

He would rather have them come to his door collecting straight-out donations. "Guiding and Scouting have always stood for moral and physical training and leadership. I am saddened to see the disappearance of these ideals."

Letters, Parent. "Be Prepared" questions the value of "Bob A Job Week" for Boy Scouts. I hold exactly the reverse opinion.

"Bob A Job Week" provides a time of cheap labour, when neglected odd jobs can be done and done well. Boys, who have been in the Scout movement over a period of years, take pride and satisfaction in a job well done and the benefit they have received from their training in Scouting would prevent most Scouts from giving anything but their best to the community.

In some cases their willingness is exploited and they are often paid less than the job is worth; e.g. cleaning out a wood shed, stacking the wood and raking the garden, two hours' work for 3/-; cleaning household silver, black from months of neglect, 2/-.

This is all in the game and nothing is lost if the job is done well, but let us realise the boys are working for the Scout movement, not themselves, and let us pay them what the job is worth.

Letters, Willing Giver. When the Girl Guides or Boy Scouts come to me for jobs, I give them a job to do which they can manage. One lad always cleans half a dozen or so pairs of shoes and is given 2/-. This is one job less for me to do.

The Girl Guide did an hour's soft ironing and earned 4/- for her efforts – another job less for me. It's up to the adults to find the right job for the Guide or Scout to do.

Letters, Guiseppe Comonsoli. Last Sunday afternoon I was woken from my nap by four youths in a military-style uniform, which I found out later was from the Scouts. To my hazy mind, I was suddenly thrown back about thirty years when Hitler's Youths patrolled the streets at weekends and performed acts of violence on people they were being trained to hate.

No matter how good a cause these lads had, it is wrong that they should parade round in uniform and come pounding on the doors of citizens.

Comment. Various bits of legislation in multiple States have almost wiped out the door-knock appeals on Sunday afternoons, and other times. At the same time, the Scouts and Guides are a lot less visible that they were in the 1960's.

MEDALS FOR THE BEATLES

Every Year, at the long weekend in June, and on New Year's Day, the Queen announced a list of Honours for eminent Australians. Some people got knighthoods, and many more got lesser honours. But in all, about 400 people every year were thus rewarded for services to the community. Of recent years, this ritual has been replaced by the Australian Honours list, and the knighthoods have been replaced by the Order of Australia, and the like, but the system is pretty much unchanged.

This year, under the British version of the system, the Beatles were each awarded an OBE, Order of the British Empire. This led to lot of head scratching as to the reason for the system in the first place, and the following Letters are typical.

Letters, Art Lover. Can someone tell me who selects persons for Queen's Honours? Obviously the Queen cannot do this personally; so who does and on what grounds are selections made?

One can, of course, argue that the Beatles provide "pleasure and enjoyment" to a large number of people; but so does alcohol, tobacco, marihuana and members of the oldest profession. Therefore, this cannot possibly be the criterion; nor can it be that in earning millions for oneself, one cannot very well avoid that in the process Great Britain gets a just share of it; so what was the criterion in the case of the Beatles?

Letters, Valerie Elliston. I am not a Beatles fan, but I feel I must speak up about the churlishness of the persons who returned their MBEs in protest at the Beatles joining their august company. One of them, we are told, was an RAF hero. One of the most important things for which he and his compatriots fought was freedom of choice, and this applies to selecting recipients of MBEs.

One of the few times I have seen the Beatles was during their televised Sydney Press interview, when they parried questions both insulting and impertinent with wit and good humour. In terms of foreign currency, publicity and entertainment the Beatles have probably done more for the United Kingdom than their detractors care to admit.

I do not approve of the standards which make this possible, any more than I approve of many other present-day values, but they exist, and will not be negated by a childish insult to the Queen and her decoration.

Letters Marjorie Penny. I hate bitter snobs, sending their medals back to the Queen because they no longer feel themselves to be in the ranks of the godly.

A different war is raging now – between hard and soft currency – and these four boys, of humble origin, have filled a small gap in that respect, as no other team could have. They do not deserve the scorn that is being poured on them. I am middle-aged, I am proud of them, love and admire them, and may God bless them.

Letters, Elina Mansfield. I don't think that an MBE was a suitable award for the Beatles, but it must be a great incentive to them to live up to it and, in doing just that, give a good example to the young people who admire them so much.

Letters, Mrs H M Gould, Cronulla. Much of what "Art Lover" says is perfectly true. **If giving pleasure, or earning millions**, thereby paying sufficient taxes to keep many Public Servants' salaries covered, **is the criteria** for receiving honours, where does it end?

I have seen no outbreak of public indignation because Betty Cuthbert was also honoured by the Queen... yet, to follow through "Art Lover's" argument, has she done more than Dawn? Or more than any other man, who spends endless patient hours teaching spastics to swim, with little thanks or recognition from any other than the spastics' parents?

I feel, since singers, dancers, cricketers and jockeys, to name just a few, have not only been given Orders, but knighthood in the past, there should be no reason to exempt the Beatles. So why the furore?

Since there is no British Empire anyway, the order seems extinct. In my humble opinion, all such honours should be eliminated in this age of democracy, for among people who care about such things, there must be much heartburning at times at the thought of being slighted.

Meantime, good luck to Betty and the Beatles and anyone else who was singled out for the Queen's blessing.

Comment. They can keep them as far as I am concerned. It's all frivolous at one level, but the idea of recognising good achievements can't be all that bad. In some cases, it would be a crying shame if no official recognition was recorded.

JULY NEWS ITEMS

News item, July 1st. Seven hundred young men **were sent off to an Army camp for three months today.** They are the first group to be drafted into **National Service** because of the **Vietnam situation**. Many mothers protested and clashed with police at Central Station, but **to the youths it was the start of a wonderful new adventure.**

Oh goodie. Progress is coming. Sydney yesterday had its first sonic boom. It came from Mirage fighters, flying out to sea. A resident of Sydney suburb Lidcombe was quoted as saying "I ran outside, and my neighbours did too. **A car stopped in the street.** It was all very terrifying. For a while I thought the whole area was blowing up."

Margaret Smith and Roy Emerson each won their **Wimbledon** singles finals over the weekend. This is **the first time that Australia has held both titles at the same time.**

In 1963, the University of New England at Armidale (NSW) decreed that **male and female students could not visit each other's colleges. Today 700 students did just that**, sitting and having tea or playing cards. The normal fine per person would be 25 Pounds for such a breach, but it remains to be seen **whether this protest forces a change in the rules**.

NSW will soon introduce new laws for the road. All **new** vehicles in future will have **blinking lights for left- and right-hand turns**. Also, they will have glowing **red lights to indicate stopping**. This will mean that drivers of new vehicles will **no longer have to use hand signals**....

Probationary licences will be introduced for new drivers. There was also talk **of compulsory blood tests** for drivers suspected of being under the influence of alcohol. **A decision on this has not yet been made.**

The Minister for Customs has announced that a Federal ban on four books had been lifted. They are:

Borstal Boy, by Brendan Behan. **Lady Chatterley's Lover**, by D H Lawrence. **Lolita**, by Vladamir Nabokov. **Confessions of a Spent Youth**, by Vance Bourjaily. The Minister added **Powdered Eggs**, by Charles Simmons, to the list.

Suggestion. You might like to get one of these books out of the local library, and **read it.** Have reading standards changed?

Lord Casey, aged 74, was announced Governor General today. He is only the **third Australian** to be appointed to the position. All other G-Gs had been from England, often from **persons of royal birth.**

President Johnston has **called up more young men in America** so that he can more than double the number of US troops in **South Vietnam. The number will be increased to 125,000. Most of them are babies.**

Twenty large groups from the medical groups and hospitals, as well as social work and the caring industries, held an inaugural session to consider **how to reduce smoking** among youths particularly. This was the first such Australia group to attempt an anti-smoking campaign on **such a large scale.** It recognised **the new concept of a strong link between smoking and cancer.** Although society generally was not yet convinced of the link.

The new fertility drug clomiphene is on trial in Australia. World-wide, women are having **multiple births**, with two sets of quins born this week. The child-birth industry is in turmoil, with some parents very keen to get the drug, and others frightened to use it for other purposes. In Australia, it **will be licensed only at four hospitals**, who will conduct trials.

THE DROUGHT

One thing I have learned from studying years of Australian newspapers in depth is that the weather can be relied on to be unreliable. Floods, and droughts, and bushfires, winds, and storms, and freak tides, and dry water holes, and dust-storms, and cicadas and grasshoppers, they all pop up randomly all over the place, and all over the period of my studies.

When they do, there are always people round that the Press can find who will say seriously that "This has been the worst thing ever" or "this is the worst it has been since grandfather was a boy". It always comes as a surprise that an area that was flooded thirty years ago is now flooded again, and that bush fires would burn out the same acres that were burned out in the past.

In 1965, the drought that was gripping the land was, however, a real drought, and a bad one. Sometimes the cries of "drought, we need help" are exaggerated and contrived, but this was a corker. Comments poured to the papers, and I provide a small sample below.

Letters, (Mrs) G Taber, Menangle.

After 35 years of farming, conserving fodder, building dams and rejuvenating tired eroded soil, my husband faces heartbreaking losses and I defy and challenge any Minister or Department to do likewise and then state that we "rely on luck and the Government to overcome the drought."

No, we rely on solid, hard work, 16-18 hours a day, including the Sabbath, never taking wages or holidays (we have had four weeks' annual holiday in 24 years of marriage), quietly taking adversity and rejoicing in the fruits of our labours, and giving our utmost to the land which Governor Lachlan Macquarie granted to our ancestor, Thomas Taber, for his service as a teacher in the colony.

There is no easy way to fight the natural elements, and all of man's ingenuity the world over has not yet beaten droughts. I am sure there are hundreds of farmers who will agree with me that Mr Cutler's statement is entirely unwarranted.

Letters, J Ainsworth-Smyth, Currabubula. Let's cut out all this talk about the cockies walking off their farms, and the need for Reserve bank action and all. It's dry all right, damn dry, but we've had 20 years of good seasons and good prices, and sold all our wheat to the Commies.

The first cocky who does walk off will be killed in the rush as his neighbours fight each other to buy the place.

Letters, W R Lavings, Eungai Creek. If J Ainsworth-Smyth has had 20 years of good seasons in wheatgrowing enjoying good fixed prices, the "cow-cockies" on the North Coast are a lot less fortunate. Should he have any desire to try his luck at cow-cockying, I can assure him farms are not much in demand in this part of the State and he could look forward to not being killed in acquiring property here, but may pass on trying to make a living on the best farm at the present time.

Surely with his wealth he also would have TV, which he should look at and see the results of the drought; and also he should study the news, especially the photos of dead sheep being burnt and the starving stock slowly dying in thousands.

To conclude might I suggest that J Ainsworth-Smyth find out for sure "that mirages are not real water," and also advise him always to wear a hat while in the sun as I am positive he must be suffering from illusions or wearing green-tinted sunglasses.

THE WHARFIES

Our Australian Press, in the major cities, is capitalistic. Of course it could hardly be otherwise given that it needed capital to start up in the first place, and then needed capital to expand. So, to put it very simply, whenever arguments involving labour versus capital came up, it has always sided with the latter. That's fair enough; I would have done the same in their shoes.

So that in the period from the start of WWII up till 1965, every industrial strike that occurred was given short shrift by these papers. In the first fifteen of these years, the coal miners were the major whipping boys, and even when men were killed and injured, the Press was saying that the miners should keep working under atrocious conditions. Since the mid-1950's, though, the mines have become more mechanised, and have stopped their constant striking, foolish and futile as it mainly was.

That left the wharfies as the scapegoat for the Press. It was kind enough to keep up a constant vendetta against the often-foolish demands of those workers just as it had done with the miners. Here however, extra automation had not caused the battles with the shipping companies to subside at all, and the old battles raged on day after day. Right now the Feds were getting very impatient for all the conflict to stop, and for the various parties to find ways to work together, but it seemed that long-term solutions were no closer that previously.

I enclose below a few Letters concerning the wharfies. I give them because they show a few small facets of the ongoing struggle. I suggest you do not try to come to grips with the whole situation as it was then. Simply look at the claims on both sides, and realise that every thing said had a long history behind it, and that behind that history was an equally long history of industrial hatred. If you come out of the section with some realisation of how near-impossible the whole matter was, then I will have done my job.

Letters, M E, Annandale. I am astounded and bewildered at the stupidity, bordering on insanity, demonstrated in this country's treatment of its wharf-labourers.

We have been reading for some time past of the banking-up of cargoes, slow turn-around of ships, and ships with no labour for loading and unloading; yet in the next sentence we read wharf-labourers being suspended for one, two or three working days. It would be Gilbertian if it were not so cruel. A recent Press statement stated that a "one working-day" suspension could mean that a man could be unemployed for a fortnight – this is a country where we are told there is "overfull" employment. How a casual worker's family can exist when the breadwinner is deprived of work for a fortnight is beyond my comprehension.

Then, again, the loss of a day's attendance money is equivalent to a fine, and it was recently stated in the Press that penalties of up to six days attendance money were imposed, equalling about 8 Pounds. To my mind this is no less than savage. Even criminals before a Court sometimes get off with a lesser fine than this.

I think it is time we started to treat the "wharfies" as human beings, and do something to improve their lot. It must be an irksome life, not knowing from one day to the next whether he will be called on to work at the weekend.

Let us have a little sympathy for these men. After all, some of us have teenage children earning as much as a wharfie, and many of them fought to make this country what it is. They have few amenities, no fringe benefits enjoyed by other workers, no pension to look forward to, no security of employment, and their long-service leave is a myth. With deferments they would have to live to be 100 to get three months. Yet everyone else gets three months (or more) after only 15 years. What has happened to the Australian slogan, "Fair go, mate!"? Does it only mean "fair go" for oneself?

Letters, T J Bellew, Secretary, Australian Stevedoring Industry Authority, Sydney. The statement by M E in his letter in yesterday's "Herald" on "a fair go for the wharf labourers" is a travesty of the facts.

For example, the fact is that 5,137 waterside workers have already received 1,256,814 Pounds in long-service leave payments. Waterside workers receive attendance money of 28/3 a day, holiday pay, sick pay, annual leave and long-service leave.

The general standard of amenities for waterside workers compares more than favourably with other industries. All this is despite the fact that waterside workers are casual workers.

In the financial year 1963/64, waterside workers in Sydney earned an average of 29 Pounds 6 Shillings for 37.6 hours a week.

Waterside workers may obtain information relating to Saturday work on Friday evening. Those engaged for work on Sundays are drawn from a special Sunday roster, instituted at the request of the Waterside Workers' Federation. An individual waterside worker can decline work on Sunday, but if he is available for Sunday work he may ascertain on the preceding Friday afternoon whether he will be required.

Many waterside workers appreciate the opportunity to work on Sunday, for which they are paid at the rate of double time and a half and receive a payment of 12 Pounds 15 shillings for the eight hours worked on the day shift.

Letters, W A Burt, Manager (Sydney Branch), The Association of Employers of Waterside Labour. M E delivered an emotional protest against the suspension of men who walked off the job. That protest should have been addressed to the officials of the Sydney branch of the WWF who by-passed both the Industrial Relations Committee and the Board of Reference machinery set up to deal expeditiously with disputes of this nature. Those officials knew that, in the face of this attitude, the Australian Stevedoring Industry Authority would have no alternative but to penalise the wharf labourers concerned.

M E, seeking to excuse the failure of the Federation to "go to the courts," said "human nature being what it is, under provocation men will act hastily and walking off the job is a natural reaction."

Under provocation? There was none. A sudden demand was made for **extra men** in gangs handling wool, meat, and certain other commodities, the gang sizes for the handling of which had been accepted for nine years. When this abrupt demand was not conceded, no attempt was made to have recourse to conciliation: work stopped.

In the course of the recent compulsory conference called by Mr Justice Gallagher, the employers suggested that consideration should be given to a scheme for permanent employment on the waterfront. The WWF refused even to discuss the matter.

Perhaps M E will react to the same plea: "Fair go, mate."

Letters, Lawrence Saunders. I laugh at the suggestion that the wharfies have a hard time to live. Apart from the more than ample pay, they earn a fortune from pilfering. Watch them come out with their clothes bulging with stolen treasures and you will have no doubts. Some of them stop and visit the gate-keepers who are supposed to be stopping this theft. You will find that it is then the gate-keepers whose clothes are bulging.

Comment. Sometimes I think we all despair when public disputes go on and on, over generations sometimes, for no apparent reasons. We all know of the Jews and Arabs, and the Catholics and Protestants in Ireland, for example. Here, on a smaller scale, it seemed that this problem too was intractable.

As it turned out, though, over a period of many years, a better way was found, as all parties gave a little. In 2019, now, the wharfs are as peaceful as they have ever been. Granted, we have seen some titanic struggles and head-on confrontations within the last 20 years, but still the niggling day-on day-off performance has given way to a more controlled way of settling the inevitable disputes.

SOME BRAVE NEW IDEAS

I should mention a few new ideas that were steadily grabbing a hold on society. I enclose a few Letters that give only one aspect of each of them, just to remind you that they weren't always as widely accepted as they are now.

Home Unit Rush

Mr Geoffrey Morgan complained of the relentless spread of home unit buildings over Sydney's lower north shore, "with no consideration whatsoever for the wishes of residents who want to preserve their homes, gardens and families in these suburbs."

He quotes Selwyn Street, Wollstonecraft, a charming tree-lined street of largish houses that has been selected for the creation of three-storey and up to eight-storey blocks of units. He says residents just want to be left in peace in our homes. "Homes have been created by home-owners over many years, and they are destroyed by developers in one year."

Comment. I wonder what Mr Morgan would say if he looked at parts of all Oz cities now.

Poker Machine Returns

Poker machines have been here a long time. In the war years and aftermath, they appeared in clubs and parlours as fruit machines, and while they were very hard to get money out of, their incidence had not yet grown to the stage where they were considered a social problem.

By the mid-sixties, however the management of the machines, and the avarice of their promoters, was starting to look like big business. At the same time, the number of players had increased as they had permeated Workers, and football, and RSL Clubs, and some measure of control was being called for.

Letters, Victim. Since poker machine licensing is apparently here to stay and the devices are to continue to operate legally, surely it is time that a uniform set of conditions should be laid down.

At present there is no fixed scale of "return" to the player, payouts being at the whim of the particular club where machines are installed. In some cases a return of up to 90 per cent is policy; in others "jackpots" are small and infrequent and other small dividends are equally scarce. Some of the machines should be labelled "strictly for amusement only" so scanty are the returns to the player. This seems irresponsible. Surely if the State Government is to continue licensing the "bandits" as a taxing device, payouts should be standardised in all respects.

A National Health Scheme

There was a lot of current talk about the Federal Government paying for the entire health system. This would be along the lines of the then-British system, where all costs were sheeted home to the government. In theory it paid the wages of doctors and the costs of hospitals and for drugs.

There were obvious problems with this approach. For example, it would promote over-use of the system by patients who then had no reason to economise on the services they sought. But such arguments **here** were going round and round, and, unless I am mistaken, are still doing so.

The British system at the time was seriously advocated for Australia. Here is an idealised view of the benefits.

Letters, Doctor. The assumption that Australian doctors do not want a British-type national health service as stated in your Editorial of July 2 may not be based on the views of a large number of doctors. In fact some form of modified health scheme may be the very answer to many of the problems now besetting this persistently maligned profession.

The most obvious benefit from a national health service would be an end to bad debts which plague medicine as in no other occupation. Less obvious would be the effect on general practice. Most Australian doctors would, I am sure, find general practice under the shambles of the British system so repugnant that those at present engaged therein would leave, and most young doctors graduating would studiously avoid this medical anachronism and head straight for the specialities already fast supplanting general practice as the first line of medical treatment.

Such time-consuming and wasteful procedures as **home consultations would cease** to exist, and with them much mumbo jumbo better suited to witchdoctors than modern-day medicos. Medicine would then be practised where it belong – in hospitals, and by adequately trained specialists. **The old cry of doctor-patient relationship would be heard, but, really, how important is this?** A hangover from the days when medicine was an "art," it is now as necessary as sails on a ship. The "human" touch can satisfactorily be handled by almoners – once again, specialists in their own particular field.

The service would allow reasonable off-duty for doctors, something at present enjoyed neither by those in private practice nor those working in hospitals, as the resultant extra hospital staff recruited from the now defunct general practices would at last be adequate. The most abused facet of medicine at the moment, namely that doctors "on call" at night are on duty by day as well, would end, the extra ranks providing enough doctors for a night duty rota to be as workable as in any 24-hour industry.

Finally, a national health service would permit those persons desiring private medical services to arrange such with a physician unencumbered by the annoyances of medical benefit regulations.

Comment. You might pick up that Doctor's thinking was a bit clouded by the benefits he saw. He was short on details of the mechanics of how the changes might come about in a real world. But his Letter is typical of those produced on this matter at the time, and most of them were full of generalities, with no evidence of being based on fact or logical thought processes.

Abolition of Hand Signals

Finally, in this Section, I enclose a Letter prompted by the newly announced decision to scrap hand signals.

Letters, L Griffith. May I, as a Victorian who has experienced the dangers of motoring without "stop" hand signals, make a plea that the NSW authorities think twice before introducing such a stupid measure?

It is ridiculous to argue that stop lights on a car are sufficient. **They do not operate until the brakes are actually being applied**, which gives no period of warning to those following. A correctly-given hand signal gives ample warning to a following driver to take action.

Abolition of the stop signal by hand can only lead to more road smashes, and consequently higher insurance premiums. I have driven in all States, and consider that the observance of road manners in this State to be far better than in others, so please keep it that way. Stick to the hand signal.

Letters, M F Dixon. The proposal to abolish drivers' hand signals in NSW takes no account of the value of the stop hand signal to pedestrians in the act of crossing a road or street, whether at a pedestrian crossing or not.

Responsible drivers, when approaching pedestrians, invariably give the stop hand signal to indicate they are slowing down or stopping, according to their distance from the pedestrian. This tells the pedestrian he has been seen and that it is safe for him to proceed. Without this signal he has no means of knowing what the driver intends to do and becomes uncertain what he himself should do – and I think all drivers will agree that a confused or uncertain pedestrian is a menace to all road-users, including himself.

The proposal to abolish hand signals may be all right for following motorists who have brake lights to guide them, but without the stop hand signal the pedestrian in front will have nothing to indicate what an approaching driver intends to do.

Letters, A P Rigby. For pedestrians crossing at pedestrian crossings, it is absolutely essential for the motorist to signify his intention to stop. If lights are to supersede hand signals, they should be at front and rear of cars and of a distinctive colour, not of the red or yellow variety.

Comment. Come to think of it, some of them are right. How do forward pedestrians work out if you are going to stop?

AUGUST NEWS ITEMS

The Australian Labour Party, at the Federal level, is in some turmoil. **The right wing is trying to reduce the influence of Trade Unions in the Party**, while the Left wing wants it to stay the same….

Arthur Calwell, the Party's leader, is in the Left wing, and **his Deputy, Gough Whitlam, is growing in stature**, and is pressing towards challenging for the leadership. **More will be heard of this young man.**

Australian swimmer, **Linda McGill**, aged 19, **successfully swam the English Channel**. She was 19 minutes outside the record for women, and **the first Australian female to do so.**

August 10th. **Singapore** rather secretly announced that it **had broken with Malaysia, and had become an independent state**. Britain will retain her military base there. Unsettling in a troubled region, and a lot of question marks….

Students from Malaysia and Singapore are dismayed by the move. The Singapore students are left with passports and visas that might be of no use to them. As well, there is now a split with Malaysian students who were previously of the same nation….

August 11th. **Australia gave diplomatic recognition to the new nation of Singapore.**

August 14, news item. **Los Angeles** was engulfed over the weekend by **negro rioters**. **About 30 of them were killed**, and an uneasy quiet was restored to the city by tens of thousands of police and National Guard troops. The riots were caused by an aggregation of claims that negroes were being discriminated against. The rioters at times pinned down the police and firemen by sniper rifle fire….

US families across the nation opened their Sunday papers to see photos of National Guardsmen in **steel helmets charging rioters with fixed bayonets**, manacled and bloody prisoners forced to lie face-down on the streets, and visions of the **berserk negro mobs who for four nights had burnt and pillaged**. The riots spread to other parts of California.

It's all very exciting. **The Queen Mother will visit Oz early next year.** The republicans were still hardly heard in Oz.

The rents on most houses in Oz had been fixed since about 1941 by Commonwealth powers. The idea at the time was to stop profiteering, and to keep inflation under control. But in most States, **the prices were still frozen at 1941 levels. This was great for the tenants, but terrible for the landlords....**

Over the years, and across the States, various attempts had been made to bring rents more into line with the value of money. Still, the inequitable position mainly prevailed. **Politicians knew that renters outnumbered landlords, and they would lose net votes if they changed things....**

There were various moves afoot **now** to raise rents, and there was no doubt that sanity would one day prevail. **But which day?**

Long hair in young men was becoming popular. A Doctor Brian Entwisle startled a few parents when he said that "**long hair on the forehead and neck has contributed to many severe attacks of acne.**"

The Pope of the Roman Catholic Church was Paul VI. In 1965, he closed Vatican II, which had been set up, by John XXIII to bring reforms to the Church. Paul VI tried to use Vatican II to make a few serious reforms, but conservative elements blocked many moves. **Final score: Conservatives: some. Liberals: about the same.**

RIGHT ON THE BUTTON

Remember a few months ago we had a lot of citizens complaining about Scouts and Guides cutting into their snooze time on Sunday afternoons? Well, there was another menace that added its fair share to the general irritation.

Buttons, about an inch in diameter and stuck into your lapel, were becoming a plague. The idea was that some organisation, quite often with a worthy cause, wanted to raise money, and thought that the best way to do that was to badger people on the streets for a donation, and to give them in exchange a small useless token button.

This meant that on certain days, depending on the State, the street was blockaded with volunteers who wanted money. In some States, they were restricted. For example, by 1965, in Sydney they could only appear on Fridays. But in any case, you could guarantee that in any length of city street, you would have to fight off the well-meaning folk intent on skewering you in the breast.

Agitation to gain control was under way.

Letters, Sam Sismey. I have created my own button, twice as big as the normal button on sale. On it I have printed "I do not buy buttons." It deters half the button-hawkers. But the fat, overdressed ones are so bound up in their own goody-goody image to read anything.

Letters, Ron Curry. I bought a button on Friday, and put in on my lapel. Then a few minutes later, I was accosted by another woman who argued that the button I bought was a cheap one, and that a man so well-dressed should buy a dearer one. There was no point in telling her that the only reason I bought a button at all was to be rid of her and her type, but she insisted I buy the expensive button. I regretfully had to tell her to get out of my way, and stop being a public nuisance.

Letters, H Bedwin, President, Civilian Maimed and Limbless Association, Camperdown. I read with some dismay that the City Council had decided that eleven charities only would be allocated button days in 1966. All other charities would share nine days between them.

Apart from my concern for the threatened financial loss to our organisation, I feel that the City Council has inferred that the 11 charities named are in some way superior and this tends to cast a reflection on other charities. Although I love animals, I find it galling to see priority given to the RSPCA before organisations catering for human beings whose needs are still unmet within our community.

Button-selling is one of the few ways in which a struggling charity can achieve a financial result by its own efforts without getting into the hands of professional fund-raisers.

Letters, (Dr) Gerard Campbell. Isn't it about time the fortunate people of this prosperous country abolished charity? Let the fortunate many pay for the unfortunate few.

A disability tax paid yearly would do away with the irritation of button-day parasites who wax fat collecting from door to door, "experts" who think up bigger and better ways to bleed the man in the street, socialite committees and boring charity balls.

Charity is degrading, both for those who give and those who receive. Let **the people of Australia** shoulder the burden of the blind, the lame, the spastic and the mentally defective.

I will be quite willing to pay my disability tax in advance.

Letters, A Hayes. I question the premise on which the City Council based its decision to limit button days in the city.

If newspaper reports are correct, preference was given to the organisations which have had **the most successful button days in the past**. What an ill-conceived criterion. The lack of logic in the method is illustrated by the fact that an organisation interested in the welfare of animals has been allocated a button day in preference to many organisations caring for handicapped people.

BETTER DEAL FOR PUNTERS

The TAB was available in all States so that punters could have a bet on the horses, dogs and trots. These TABs were new State-run ventures, and operated under different rules depending on the State. But they were all much of a muchness and, being completely new, were rather experimental, and were ready to adopt changes as their experiences dictated.

In NSW, the minimum betting unit had been fixed at two shillings and sixpence initially. **Now**, there was a proposal to double it to five shillings. This was because most bets placed were valued at five shillings or more. This raised some comments.

Letters, Neville W Montagu. There seems to be great danger of the "poor man's betting unit" being changed from the basic 2/6 (25 cents) to a new minimum of 5/ (50 cents).

With the introduction of the 2/6 unit on the TAB, elderly people, including pensioners, could, for the first time in their lives, legally make a small wager on the animal of their choice at a price which they could afford.

The Premier, Mr Askin, has done a very good job up to date, and before he even considers such a disastrous proposition, he should make a tour of many of the TAB offices to see for himself the vast numbers of elderly people who would gradually disappear if the basic unit was increased to a minimum 5/ or 50 cents.

Letters, P T Harris. Your correspondents who are urging the Premier, Mr Askin, not to do away with the 2/6 TAB unit are all right as far as they go, but they don't go far enough.

Why should units be as high as 2/6? What chance does this give schoolchildren and toddlers to have their little flutter.

So far from abolishing the 2/6 unit, which enables pensioners and others who can't afford it to indulge their democratic right to gamble on the speed or otherwise of horses and dogs, the Government should introduce immediately a 3d unit.

The kiddies have been denied punting justice too long. A 3d unit would give the youngsters and deadbeats a chance, and lay firm foundations from which future generations of gamblers can be drawn.

Letters, D C Summers. I refer to the director of the TAB and his board's statement that they favour the increase of the 2/6 units to 5/.

Will the director of the lotteries take this lead and favour only 1 Pound lottery tickets, and finish with 5/ and 10/ lotteries?

What about the small punter? Is he going to be out on the limb; bet 5/ or else?

Another irritation for the punters came from the regulations regarding broadcasting of races. The authorities remembered that pre-TAB, punters had congregated in the back-yards of pubs during a race, listening to the race-call over the radio. The scene was often pretty disgusting, with grog, and punch-ups and cursing punters thrown wildly into the mix. So this was to be avoided.

Thus, broadcasting of races was not allowed on or near TAB premises, and this carried over to details of jockeys. The voice of the punter below echoes many others.

Letters, Walter G Judge. As a regular investor on TAB, I desire to protest against the present system of broadcasting race information and results. With the rapid growth of TAB, it is more than time to reconsider the arrangements.

Information such as a change in jockeys, withdrawal of horses, etc., is not available to the TAB punter, who relies on the radio stations for his information. There are many punters who back a horse ridden by a certain jockey, and who would not do so when aware that the animal is not ridden by the rider nominated in the newspapers.

I also protest against the policy of the Sydney Turf Club, which does not permit the broadcasting of a race while it is being run. I fail to see any reason why the Sydney Turf Club should be entitled to any portion of TAB investments under these conditions.

Considering the huge investments being made on TAB, and its potential, I suggest those in authority should take another look at the present scheme with a very open mind.

Comment. Of course **you** know that the unit was, soon after, increased up to five shillings. The restrictions on broadcasting still mainly prevail. And punters still win as much money as they ever did.

One Letter from the well-known Protestant minister Reverend Gordon Powell raised an interesting objection to TABs. He pointed out that the business community in one Sydney suburb had indicated that it did not want a new TAB in its precincts. The NSW Minister for Local Government had said that he would have no regard for their wants, and would create one in the suburb regardless. This, of course, Mr Powell saw as an establishing a policy, and he objected strongly to it.

He pointed out that many people saw TABs as moral evils, and he doubted if they would ever have been introduced into the State of NSW if a referendum had been held. He also claimed that the TAB would take money from local businesses, and rob them of revenue that they might otherwise get. Further, that gambling losses would certainly increase the number of bad debts in the retail community, and could well force some traders out of business.

Powell, along with other writers, also objected to the Minister's decision on the grounds that responsible businessmen had clearly enunciated a policy on matters that affected them. But the Minister had taken no regard of their wishes, and imposed a policy on them dictated by the interests of a centralised and impersonal government. These writers asked whether this was the way that a democracy should function, and deplored the end result that in denying the right to local determination, it had placed temptation in the way of young people and housewives and breadwinners.

Letters, G O'Connor. For years punters have had to break the law by going down dirty lanes, into hotel toilets and behind fences to have an S.P. bet at ridiculously low and unfair odds, each time risking a fine and a resultant record.

Last week a friend recommended TAB telephone betting to me. I envisaged a lot of red tape and long delay. I took out an account and code number in less than three minutes and now I can sit in safety in the cool of my veranda with the "Herald" and transistor and make my Saturday, or any racing day, a pleasant one. Congrats to TAB for a super service, utmost courtesy, latest scratching information and speedy, efficient and accurate service.

THOUGHTS ON VIETNAM

I am still intent on not using up all my space by writing about details of the war that is building up in Vietnam. But I must take a little time out to present some of the ideas that were being spawned by the conflict.

You will remember that it was basically a test of strength between **Capitalism**, led by an enthusiastic America, and **Communism**, represented by the Vietcong forces of North Vietnam and backed by the Chinese communists. We, Australia, were being seduced into the conflict by our long-standing commitment to mutual support with America.

The American notion was that the Reds were intent on taking South Vietnam under their umbrella, then after that they would gradually work their way down through Malaysia, Indonesia, and to Australia. This was the so-called Domino theory, and their ultimate goal, I have been told, was to reap domination of Tasmania.

This view, however, was just one of many that kept popping up. I give you a sample of the writings on the subject, and warn you that a full coverage would take quite a few books.

Letters, Arthur Summers. Some of your correspondents show a remarkable selectivity in their protests on the conduct of the war in Vietnam. Mrs E B Gale, Dr R Tirrell and J Myles have expressed their horror at the actions of

South Vietnamese troops and the Americans, presumably at the use of napalm.

Did Mrs Gale feel sick in the stomach when she read that American and South Vietnamese airmen shot down and who are not killed on the spot expect to suffer a slow death after castration and evisceration?

Has Dr Tirrell been revolted by the murdering of more than 2,000 South Vietnamese officials and civilians during the past 18 months in a terror campaign to gain control of the population? Or at the recent massacre in Saigon's My Canh floating restaurant?

If they haven't felt revulsion at these things, then there must be something wrong with them. If they have, then why haven't they protested at these atrocities, instead of only protesting against our allies?

Americans are giving their lives and their wealth to defend South Vietnam, though there is nothing in it for them. If America withdraws from Vietnam, American herself will still be secure. For Australia, however, it would prove that South Vietnam now – and her neighbours later – are expendable. Obviously self-preservation dictates that we should be striving with all our might to back America up, not trying to pull her down.

Letters, Frederick Aarons, Exeter. The intransigence of the North Vietnam Government in making withdrawal of US process a "prerequisite" for armistice negotiations raises the awful probability that the bloody and profitless conflict in South Vietnam may be continued indefinitely and with increasing violence. For the United States to evacuate South Vietnam would not only be a humiliation and loss of prestige in the eyes of the world – of the Asiatic world in particular – it would, in the judgment of Washington, mean the abandonment of Indo-China and Thailand to the tender mercies of Chinese Communism.

But what of the alternative? If the USA and her allies force an armistice by sheer weight of military power and insist upon a "democratic" form of government in Saigon, what assurance will the long-suffering people of Vietnam have that an honest capacity to govern them will be any more apparent in the future than it has been in the past.

The immediate problem, however, is neither political nor military – it is a challenge to human integrity to halt the slaughter.

Letters, (Mrs) J Hilliard. It seems to be a fairly widely held opinion that, whilst many Vietnamese do not particularly wish to be ruled by Saigon, they also have no wish to be ruled by Communism.

In other words, they want freedom to choose their own Government.

At least this much is certain: if America and her allies win the present struggle in Vietnam then, indeed, the South Vietnamese will have the freedom to choose.

If the Communists win then the South Vietnamese will have as much freedom to elect the Government of their choice as have the people of Hungary, China, East Germany and all the other "liberated" nations.

For this reason, and for the sake of our own future, we should support America's efforts to the limit of our ability.

Letters, A L Mackay. In F C Robinson's letter he mentions SEATO and in doing so he raises two questions.

When is the request of South Vietnam for military assistance to be tabled in Parliament as requested by the Opposition? If there are military obligations under SEATO, how is it that the UK, France, Pakistan, Thailand and the Philippines have not found it necessary to honour them?

RESPECT FOR THE VIETCONG

The Editor of the *SMH* on July 21 started out with some good common sense. He was commenting on the sentencing of guards of the WWII German Camp at Auschwitz. He examined their motivation in participating in very cruel practices, and went on to say that it is **possible for kindly people to commit fiendish acts of cruelty once you persuade them that their victims are not quite human**.

He said that once the Nazis had persuaded the Germans that the Jews were an inferior race, the rest was only too easy. Likewise, in South Africa with the blacks, and in Queensland and Tasmania with our own blacks. He added that it helped to give your victim a derisive name, like yid, boong, wop or dago.

He then got himself into hot water with a few readers. He claimed that we were doing this in Vietnam, by referring to our opponents there as **Commos,** and that we saw them as small, yellow, and therefore different. He agreed that Communism there was indeed a threat to us, but that **we should not forget that the Communists were also human.** "The Vietcong deserve the respect which our soldiers have always felt for the enemy against whom they fought."

This was a bit much for some readers. The Oz population had not yet had the inevitable atrocity stories of a full-scale Vietnam war, and our few casualties had been sometimes self-inflicted, but still we were in an unofficial war, and our men were very much at risk. It was a big ask to suggest that all readers should turn the Christian cheek to the Vietcong.

Letters, F McElhone. The "Herald" in its leading article headed "Greatest crime in history" rightly condemns the extinguishing of some millions of Jews by Nazi Germany on racial grounds. In the last part of the article you quite irrelevantly refer to and show inexplicable sympathy towards the Communists. You qualify this to some extent by saying, "Communism in Asia is a serious threat to Australia." You, in effect, object to Communists being called "Commos." They, however, in their propaganda and otherwise have for years used the most abusive and insulting language against those opposed to or exposing them.

Again you say, "We should not forget that Communists are also human." It is they and not we who have forgotten that people are human. Wherever Communists have come to power, they have done so by force and maintained it similarly, often with the greatest barbarism and brutality, of which there are numerous examples.

Letters, Penelope Moulden. Your editorial ends with the statement that "the Vietcong deserve the respect which our soldiers have always felt for the enemy against whom they fought." After having carefully reminded us that Asian Communists are also human beings, do you call it "respect" to hunt down and kill the Vietcong or do you mean that our soldiers should respect those Vietcong who are hardy enough to survive the Australians' famous fighting prowess?

I think the latter must be what you mean or you could not condone the participation of the Australian forces in the Vietnam war. Certainly, if the Vietcong reduces itself to using a sub-human method such as terrorism to obtain its political goals, then South Vietnam has every right to get its friends to help.

In this case, sub-human aims are destroyed by sub-human methods and the civilised word "respect" has nothing to do with either. In the long run, success in war depends on how many of the enemy you can kill, so **respect for humanity must surely be eradicated from any soldier's mind if he is going to be successful.**

Respect for people of different races and political creeds will only come about with much more person-to-person contact under peaceful conditions. To me, contact between ordinary people from both sides is the important first step of progress towards civilised respect for humanity. It is up to the Immigration Department to make this possible.

SEPTEMBER NEWS ITEMS

The Army said that, in the last six months, it had **accepted 1801 recruits from 6037 volunteers**. Less than a third of applicants were fit enough.

American entertainer P J Proby excited the young girls at the Sydney Stadium. **P J WHO, did you ask?** Well, he was mobbed, knocked to the stage, cuddled, and screamed at by hundreds of hysterical girls. **He was wearing skin-tight lilac pants, which had taken him 15 minutes to put on.** He had a matching loose lilac blouse, and a similar hair ribbon, and high-heeled satin shoes. Of course, he had long hair….

The point is that this was **the era of mayhem among maidens** who had their hours of screaming enjoyment at any young American who flew into any city in Oz and performed. Those girls are now aged about 65. **Were any of my readers there?**

September 7th. As if we did not have enough conflict in our region with Vietnam and Malaysia-Indonesia animosities, **India has now invaded Pakistan**. No one will ever remember what caused the invasion, but both sides will say they are in the right.

An intoxicated gentleman in Adelaide was refused another drink. He took a **wad of 10-Pound notes from his pocket, and tore them up**, saying "they are no good to me in here." He was charged in Adelaide Police Court with **wilfully mutilating Australian bank notes**.

American Republican Richard Nixon, ex vice-President of the US, was in Canberra and at the National Press Club. He **had been in Oz in 1953, and the Press did not like him then**. A veteran Pressman described him then. "He left me with the impression of a bumptious, almost arrogant, over-assertive smart-alec American politician"….

The same journalist today said "**we are seeing a new Nixon today. A mature, mellow Nixon**. The man has even acquired wit and humility. Somewhere along the way, Tricky Dicky has lost his bag of tricks." **Obviously, a reformed trustworthy character.**

News item, September 11th. **Australia is getting more involved in Vietnam.** Today, an aircraft carrier will leave for there. It will carry 350 men, and loads of aircraft for battle.

September 18th. Saint George Rugby League Club beat South Sydney in the Grand Final. **This was the 10th successive Grand Final victory for St George.**

News item, September 22nd. **Lord Casey was sworn in as Governor General** by the Chief Justice in the High Court, Sir Garfield Barwick. Casey was the **first Australian-born** Governor General **appointed by a non-Labour government.**

The Federal Government announced **measures in Parliament that would reduce the power of the Waterside Workers Federation (WWF).** It intends to remove the recruiting function of the WWF, and give it to the Australian Stevedoring Industry Authority. This would stop **the WWF from recruiting only family and mates (sometimes criminals?) to its ranks....**

A second provision would also leave the WWF more open to **discipline by the Government**. It can be expected that **the WWF will get quite upset by these moves, but will see that it is pointless in opposing them, given the Government is so resolute.**

By 1965, where had all the hairy-dog jokes gone? Remember those hoary old punchlines?

THE WHITE AUSTRALIA POLICY

A Special Feature in the *SMH* examined the WAP. It noted that it was still very much in force, and though it had been liberalised since the disastrous days of Arthur Calwell, it was current policy. But today it had a somewhat different flavour.

For example, family reunion was more readily accepted than 15 years earlier. Some Asians, from British Empire countries, gained admittance, but not if they were of a darker colour. Shipping companies in England would not accept bookings from coloured or partly coloured would-be passengers, though they could be "cleared" by Australia House. Exceptions were made occasionally.

Thus, a black American gentleman called Dean Dixon got clearance. But then, he was a famed musician and he came here to be resident conductor of the Sydney Symphony Orchestra. Other "highly meritorious and distinguished" people were allowed in, but look at their numbers. Only 14 in 1962, 16 in 1963, and 16 in 1964.

Thus, apart from an insignificant number of exceptions, the WAP was still Australia's enforced policy. The non-European minority of our population has fallen from 3 percent in 1861 to 0.3 per cent in 1961.

The Feature goes on to say that the general population is more accepting of coloureds than our official position would suggest. It quotes a recent Gallup poll that said that 5 per cent of people favoured **unrestricted** immigration by Asians. **But** it found that 73 percent **wanted to let in small numbers**. Only 22 percent hoped to keep out Asians altogether. This is a big change from even 10 years earlier.

The Feature sums up. "Australian authorities are retreating from the WAP by stealth. The policy, though, remains one of the most racist and exclusivist in the world. It is trying to get rid of the term "White Australia", while keeping the reality behind it. The question is: Who's fooled?"

Comment. A wide variety of opinions followed the Article.

Letters, J Heagney. It seems undeniable that the collapse of the Malaysian Federation is in some measure due to the **fear, distrust and antagonism** felt by the **Chinese and Malay elements of the population for each other.**

The opponents of the White Australia policy would have Australia accept as immigrants quite large numbers of Malays and Malaysian Chinese. It seems to me that this would **transfer the Malay-Chinese struggle to a new arena.** While it is true that this transplanted hostility would be on a comparatively small scale, it would I feel, be large enough and real enough to disturb the peace and to prevent these people becoming Australians.

I submit, therefore, that the practice of White Australia is not untowardly selfish or un-Christian. It is a realistic and necessary means of keeping out of Australia conflicts and hatreds made in Asia.

Letters, L Matheson. It would appear from the trend of the commentary by Craig McGregor on the White Australia policy that he favours the abandonment of this policy by using the thin edge of the wedge by increasing migration of coloured people.

In spite of the hostility that White Australia has caused in Asian countries and the fact that we live on the edge of a coloured continent, it would appear to be a safer course to declare to the world that experience elsewhere has shown that white and coloured races simply cannot live cheek by jowl without open hostility, resulting in damage to property, bloodshed and even murder, becoming part of our lives.

To open the migration gates and to subject Australians to the shocking racial disturbances that regularly make the headlines from other parts of the world would be the greatest act of folly, and those responsible for it would warrant the condemnation they would surely receive.

It might be said that Australians would be more tolerant of coloured people, but we have not yet been put to a real test because our contact, even with our own Aborigines or with other "coloureds," has been so limited as to raise little hostility. The real test will come with the gradual watering-down of the White Australia policy. Despite Asians' hostility to it, we should retain it and state clearly our reasons for it.

Letters, O D Bisset. Most people will agree with Craig McGregor that we should drop the so-called White Australian Policy, but I am quite sure that the overwhelming majority of Australians feel strongly that our immigration policy should be so designed that everything possible is done to avoid involving us in the kind of racial tension that is plaguing Ceylon, Fiji, British Guiana, Cyprus, Belgium, Canada, India, Pakistan, Uganda, the Congo, the Sudan, USA, and, unhappily, Great Britain.

It will be noted that in the first 11 of these countries the tension has nothing to do with the colour of men's faces.

As for the suggestion so often made that we should admit a quota of educated trained people from Asian and African countries, we could hardly do those countries a greater disservice than **to deprive them of the very type of people they so desperately need themselves**.

Letters, James Cavanagh. Australia's restrictive migration policy means exactly what it implies. It is restrictive, not exclusive as your correspondent Craig McGregor suggests, and sensible rather than racist.

When taxed by "distinguished and highly qualified" Asians about our "racist and exclusive" migration policy, I have either exhibited my passport showing the visa of their country or tactfully inquired how would I go about obtaining nationality in their country. Most change the subject very swiftly, a few discuss it rationally and from these few discussions I have learned much.

I am not upholding our restrictive migration policy on the grounds of colour but from concern for the future. Ceylon, Fiji, Singapore, the United States provide very sad examples of the difficulties that can arise from multi-racism. It should be remembered that in Ceylon the trouble is between Ceylonese and Tamils, yet these two people are basically from the same race. The rioting Negroes of Los Angeles and other towns in the United States are American citizens, many of them for generations back. The troubles in Fiji and Singapore are among the so-called middle social groups.

Nationhood implies the right to decide who will enter a country and under what conditions. Australia cannot abrogate this right by treaty with another country just because some of its people express a wish to come to Australia. The "distinguished and culture" minority who would grace Australia belong to a form of international set who have no loyalties of any sort. They would have none to Australia when it suited them to move on. The great majority of Asians have little interest in Australia and less desire to come here.

Hard cases must be ignored. They always make bad law. Worse when applied to migration policies. A migration policy must be administered with firmness tempered with a little charity when really necessary.

Letters, A Digger. In Burma, in the War, I saw 24 Australians die in the same battle that killed 24 Indians. There are no whiter men in this world than those Indian soldiers.

Letters, P. Leach. We cannot possibly keep out the Asians for much longer. If we keep rejecting them, they will find a way to force their entry. This might come to war, or it might not. But let us do it peacefully and according to our own rules. Else it will be forced on us somehow.

Letters, Faye Moyles. Are we so sure that our British blood is better than Asian blood? I'm not. I think blood is blood, and people are people. I've seen hundreds of Australians who are a disgrace to this nation. Do we want to keep them? I would swap them any time for the same number of carefully screened Asians. We might get rid of the no-hoper drongo culture we now have if we can bring in enough Asians with their culture.

WHO WEARS THE PANTS?

Rev Gordon Jones delivered a sermon at the Congregational Church in Lane Cove yesterday. The subject was "The Role Where Woman Has Failed hopelessly." He spoke with regret on Fathers Day.

"Like yourselves, I am a father and being a father does not mean what it meant 50 years ago. Fifty years ago, father was head of the house. There are few fathers today who are the heads of their households.

"While woman has sought to dominate every avenue of professional, commercial and governmental life, with varying degrees of success, there is no situation where she has so miserably failed as in trying to be head of the house.

"Believe me, when father says 'Go and ask your mother', it is not the cry of a weak personality, but of a personality that has been sat on and crushed."

Comment. It may come as a surprise to you, but there were at least two persons who had something to add to his remarks.

Letters, Onlooker. The Rev C Gordon Jones' outburst on Father's Day against women being head of the house should have been aimed not at women, but at all the men who frequent the clubs of New South Wales.

Does he know just in how many homes the father is so infrequently home while the children are awake that if the mother were as unreliable the home would disintegrate?

In countless homes in Sydney where the family finances are in a mess because the father comes home penniless from the poker machines, the mother also comes under fire from the reverend gentleman because she goes to work, not as he fondly imagines to "try to dominate the business world," but to keep up a semblance of normal standards of living in the home.

Of course, children need their father's influence and interest, and in homes where he is not too busy or too lazy and shiftless to take his share of the responsibility, the husband and wife work in unison to give the family moral standards and ideals to live up to – but don't tell me or any other woman that a child or adolescent takes any notice of someone they hardly know.

Letters, R S Earle Mason. I should be desolate if all men agreed with the criticisms of the Rev C Gordon Jones.

"There are few fathers today who are heads of their houses," he said. This brands man as a complete failure in allowing such a thing to happen – and isn't it rather a proof of failure to blame another for one's own weakness.

Marriage is a partnership, therefore it should take two people to make decisions and to shoulder responsibilities.

I am afraid Mr Jones rather dislikes women.

CLUBS AND POKIES

The Governments in all States had realised by now that they could make a lot of money out of licenced clubs in the suburbs and towns right round Australia. So, every decent-sized town of 3,000 or more had some group apply for a licence for a club with poker machines, and provided they were not too disreputable, the licence was granted. So there was a proliferation of such clubs in all States.

The most common one was the RSLs. Then there were Workers Clubs, sporting clubs of all types, international clubs like the Polish, and Masons, Catholics, and others. They all had some things in common. They were cheap to join, they offered reasonable premises, they served drinks for longer hours than the nearby pubs, they offered food at a cheap price, they were mainly community managed at this stage, so they had no equivalent of the local publican. They were decent enough to take wives to, and provided heaps of games and often entertainment for both men and women. Given that the competition was sleazy dirty stand-up pubs, they were big hits, and for a few decades went from strength to strength.

I have made them seem pretty good. But from different points of view, they were not so acceptable.

Letters, H Edwards. Your correspondent R White has drawn long overdue attention to the economic excrescence of the poker machines. Registered clubs are spreading like a rash over the State and the ubiquitous poker machine which makes their opulence so apparent, to the accompaniment of bad debts in other sectors of the community, should be speedily investigated and reasonable curbs put on their operation.

I live in close vicinity to a registered club. The residential area is compelled to put with their seven-day-a-week, 10-12 hour a day trading, to the detriment of those who are made to suffer drunken departures, screeching of cars late at night, the quiet of the Sabbath regularly invaded. Why isn't the law amended to bring these drinking and gambling dens, masquerading as "clubs," into line with hotel trading hours?

As for bad debts, one only has to have business interests in most of the districts in which these clubs operate to know how money is being siphoned off from legitimate needs and obligations to pay for the grog and gambling fiesta.

Letters, G W Wintle, Secretary-manager, Souths Junior Rubgy League Club. R White refers to the "evil" of poker machines and their effect on retail business.

Does Mr White think that the country suffers if the clubs build more premises? Surely it's a matter of simple economics when money is spent on buildings. Surely the brickie, the carpenter, the plumber, the painter, the labourer get some benefit by way of wages, or is it a surplus amount of money to the already "wealthy" brickie, carpenter, painter, labourer, etc.?

Surely Mr White can't mean that these gentlemen don't spend what they earn from club buildings and improvements on the butcher, the baker, the candlestick-maker? Surely Mr White doesn't think that clubs have hidden reserves – if they had, what would they be for?

As an "expert witness," and my opinion has the hallmark of experience, I say that social cubs as we know them are an impetus to the economy of the State.

Company and traders' profits are words Mr White uses very glibly. Where do profits go to? I would say to wealthy shareholders who build up big bank balances.

Mr White's arguments tend to intolerance and religious bigotry when he uses the word "evil" and his arguments about non-productive organisations are rather odd. Is every organisation to be productive in pounds, shillings and pence to shareholders? Isn't it productive to give enjoyment and pleasure, or should we be at home with the fowls when the sun goes down?

Letters, W Jennings. No matter how one may try to "whitewash" the economic effects of the poker machine, it remains fundamentally a social excrescence, and ultimately no good can come from the financing of lavish clubs from poker-machine profits.

G W Wintle considers that clubs are economic because the building of them provides wages for tradesmen and others. He neglects to add that the money to build these clubs is extracted by poker machines from the pockets of the people of the community, including these very same workers.

At present the nation is enjoying a boom period, but the occurrence of a serious recession would be disastrous for many clubs, their maintenance resting precariously on poker-machine profits. It is economically unwise in the extreme that large amounts of the State's resources should be used to build clubs whose finances have such an unreliable basis.

Comments. About 30 years ago, State governments started to introduce tougher drink-driving laws. Since then they have gradually turned the screws so that the .05 level of alcohol in the bloodstream is the legal limit for driving.

This killjoy situation, that saved many lives, spelt the death-knell for many of the smaller clubs. Bowling clubs, and RSL clubs and others folded across the nation. It is hard to see them recovering.

GIVE THE YOUNG'UNS A BREAK?

At various times throughout this book, I have cited the behaviour of teenagers, and given an implicit tut-tut to their actions. But, fortunately, there are plenty of Letter-writers ready to remind me that the youth of this nation were in fact generally a fine lot, and that the bad behaviour of some is what gets reported in the Press, and the better behaviour of the masses goes unnoticed.

Letters, Bella Cooper. As one of many, I have condemned the young lads who wear long hair, but selling badges for legacy has certainly caused me to change my mind.

During a whole day at Wynyard station, I did not see one long-haired lad without a badge. They came in groups and bought freely, but many staid gentlemen made me disgusted the way they answered when asked to buy.

Letters, Parent. Having heard so much about teenage delinquency, I went to Sydney Stadium last Saturday to the visiting folksingers' show. My real motive was to see the delinquents and I was fully prepared with my "tut tuts" and "shames" and "what's the world coming to!"

There were about 11,000 in the audience, the age group being, I would guess, from 14 to 24, excluding my middle-aged self and a few others. There were the few beards and other eccentricities but, and this is the burden of my letter, there was nothing but exemplary behaviour.

The audience received the artists with spirited courtesy, enthusiastic applause and delightful participation when intended, and the interval showed 11,000 kids stretching from their uncomfortable "seats," buying their soft drinks and sweets and being thoroughly happy. After the show the audience dispersed in an orderly manner and I particularly noticed the complete absence of pushing and jostling. In all, the whole exercise was an example of model behaviour.

Comment. I should add that all those Scouts and Guides, were good stamps as well. And so too were the teen-age button sellers. They might get annoying to some, but if that's the worst they do, they are part of a fine breed.

So, to square up my account, **if you were one of these**, you can have my pat on the back.

HIGH JINKS IN PARLIAMENT

On September 30th, a gentleman called Gough Whitlam was roundly abusing another gentleman, Paul Hasluck, in our national Parliament. There was nothing unusual in this, because this is what they get paid to do.

Hasluck took exception to what Whitlam was saying, and leaned over that table between the two men, and uttered some remark. Whereupon, **Whitlam threw a glass of water into the face of Hasluck.**

The House went into uproar, and after the shouting from both sides of the House died down, Hasluck was prevailed upon to apologise for his remark.

This incident is all the more interesting because Mr Whitlam was later to become Prime Minister of the nation. Mr Hasluck was to become Governor General at the same time. (But Hasluck's term expired just before the Whitlam crisis of 1975. The GG at **that** time was Sir John Kerr.)

Hasluck's remark was that Whitlam was "one of the filthiest objects ever to come into this Parliament".

OCTOBER NEWS ITEMS

A small baby died of natural causes in a Sydney suburb and her mother decided to hide this. She dumped the baby in the bush. **She told the police and Press that it had been kidnapped.** After two weeks of frantic searching, **the authorities found the body with the help of a visionary.** The woman was charged with obstructing the police ….

The visionary was a 64-year-old man who claimed he discovered his powers in 1927, and had helped police several times since then. **He led the police directly to the site of the body, and there is no suggestion that he was involved in any way.** He intends to make a claim for the 1,000 Pounds reward for finding the body. **The question remains: How did he do it? Does he indeed have visionary powers?**

Our very own Prime Minister was granted **a great honour by the British.** He was awarded **the honorary title of Lord Warden of the Cinque Ports (Hastings, Romney, Hythe, Dover and Sandwich).** This carried no emoluments, no duties, no residence, and in fact, **it carried nothing, just the honour.** He welcomed it, and indeed it showed how highly the British thought of him. Still, **here,** there were some irreverent people who thought it was a bit useless.

Empire Day, or more recently Commonwealth Day, **on May 24 has been a half-holiday for school children** in NSW and other States, **since 1902. It is followed by Cracker Night.** Now however, from next year, **this half-holiday will no longer be granted.** This is part of a move to cut down on the casualties caused by the growing misuse of fireworks.

Famous American Journalist Walter Lippman **on the military position in Vietnam:** "The war in Vietnam is like **punching a full tub of water.** We can make a hole with our powerful fist wherever we punch the water. But once we pull back our hand, the hole disappears."

Apparently, some **big horse race will be held early in November**. Probably in Melbourne, I hear. **It is already quite a nuisance** because the normal newspaper fare of misery and impending doom is not getting through because of it. I will find out what it's all about, and let you know.

It was announced that **Prince Charles will study for a term at the Timbertop branch of Geelong Grammar school**. He will start on February 1st, and will have his own flat, though he will eat with the other students. He will be 17 next month.

The severe drought in NSW was relieved by good rains that lasted a week, without bringing floods.

The Prime Minister has bought a house in Melbourne. The house is in the leafy old suburb of Malvern. He had been living in the Prime Minister's Lodge in Canberra since 1949. This is seen as **an indication that he will resign from his position** in the near future, although his office denies this. **In fact, he did resign before the elections in 1966.**

More than 60 people were arrested in Sydney **during a demo against our participation in the Vietnam war.** The number of demos round the nation was growing week by week.

H G Palmer, Australia's biggest electrical dealer, has been placed in the hands of a receiver, pending bankruptcy. Palmers have **143 stores nation-wide**, and much of its finance came from the public's purchase of debentures and shares. The value of these debentures is now uncertain.

Britain's leading model, Jean Shrimpton, **the Shrimp**, arrived in Oz on October 31. **She will be the guest of the Victoria Racing Club** at that big race next week. Little does she know the controversy she will stir up.

OUR POMMY MIGRANTS

Migrants from Britain had been coming here in large numbers for almost twenty years. Most of them were happy they had made the big decision to come, and a small number were not. Some of the latter had returned to the Mother Country, and quite a few of these had second thoughts and migrated back again.

A dozen Letters each year reached the *SMH* from British migrants saying how bad things were here, and how bad hostel-living was. I must say, for balance, they were always met with even larger numbers saying that things were pretty good.

In any case, I offer the following unusual Letter from an Aussie who yearned for the chance to escape to a hostel and live like a migrant.

Letters, Chained. I sympathise with complaints of migrants about hostels, but unless they arrived in Australia with some savings or the wife is working, I can assure them they had better brace themselves for the time when they escape from their "convict barracks." As an Aussie, growing up with the illusion that this was the land of plenty, I am now very disillusioned after years of fighting the housing battle.

I have four children, a husband on average working man's wage of 23 Pounds, and pay a rent of 11 Pounds 11 Shillings. Now add to this electricity of 1 Pound 10 Shillings, husband's fares 2 Pounds, medical fund 5/, school fares and expenses for two children 1 Pound. This leave 6 Pounds 14 Shillings for everything else, plus endowment which I receive quarterly.

So the migrants complain about their food! Why, beef, pork and bacon are never seen in our home. Powdered milk, margarine, rice, mince, stew, and I am ashamed of the breakfasts I have to serve my hard-working husband. No extra 5 Pounds can we find to spend on extra food. No pleasure, smoking, drinking.

Oh, to take the children even to the zoo! There are no public libraries nearby and to clothe my girls "properly" for school I had to go into debt!

Dental expenses are nightmares, but thank God we so far have been a healthy family. And thank God for the sunshine of Australia, without which the days would be most unbearable.

There is no sign of any relief from this financial strain until the children finish school. How can people be expected to populate the country, as with more than two children you are in strife. The housing farce has cost this country so much by sapping the energies of so many of the postwar youth.

Give me one year in a hostel – it seems there at least I would be able to save a few pounds to put away for that rainy day, and so let me sleep more peacefully at night. So dear migrants, count the blessings you have in your present conditions.

Life will not be all smooth going once you leave the hostel.

THE GIVING OF BLOOD

Letters, O Howes. Last week the Red Cross made an emergency appeal in the Sydney area for donations of blood. Among those who queued up to give their blood I noticed several Chinese and an African. While I commend the altruism of these people in going through a somewhat unpleasant and time-consuming business, I feel that the Red Cross, and all Australians, should discourage **people of non-European stock from giving to blood banks** in Australia. Unless this is done, we Australians cannot hope to retain our racial purity, and once this is lost, it is lost for ever.

Comment. What a brave man Mr Howes was. He knew that he was in for a torrid reception, and yet he went ahead and wrote his Letter. The next day, the first two Letters thought he was joking, and were mainly concerned to have others not take it seriously.

Letters, Ronald R Winton. Presumably O Howes has his tongue in his cheek when he writes of retaining our racial purity by discouraging people of non-European stock from giving to blood banks in Australia. It reads like a satire on the nonsense the Nazis used to talk.

However, some people may take the letter seriously, so they should know that the notion is biologically absurd. From the human relations point of view, it is frankly offensive to our brothers from other countries, and is to be deplored. As an Australian of English, Scottish and Irish descent and a medical graduate, I should, if I needed a blood transfusion, accept blood from any of my fellow men with unqualified gratitude, provided the blood group was right.

Letters, Susan Orr. The letter from O Howes regarding non-European blood donors was so incredible that I was initially at a loss to ascertain whether or not he was writing seriously.

Assuming that he is totally ignorant of the techniques involved in screening all donated blood before it can be used, allow me to point out that the colour of a donor's skin makes no difference to its value in treating the sick.

If, however, this letter was written in a flippant and provocative mood – and I can hardly believe that anyone would write in such poor taste – I hope that the non-Europeans who received this ungracious criticism failed to be hurt or discouraged by it.

The next day the floodgates opened. The Red Cross said that they would welcome donors of any race. Then Mr Howes and his Letter attracted comments such as "evil Letter denying logical argument", "unequalled stupidity and ignorance", "an opinion so utterly remote from proven fact, so distasteful politically, so full of senseless pain for those who suffer under the old prejudices of a bygone age." The abuse went on and on.

I quote a few cleverer Letters, not so directly abusive.

Letters, J V Cameron. Mr O Howes may be unaware that a similar undesirable effect is caused by non-Europeans breathing European air. I suggest that Mr Howes looks after his own purity by wearing at all times a long plastic raincoat, gloves, and leggings, inserting his head into a large plastic bag and drawing the cord around his neck.

Letters, E D Poppleton. I was delighted to read the letter of Mr O Howes on the question of the indiscriminate use of blood in transfusions. I myself make a practice of carrying on my person a small card which bears the legend, "In case of accident, administer blood of group X, sub-group WASPUGRENS."

For those uninitiated, the initials stand for White Anglo-Saxon Protestant University Graduate Resident of the North Shore.

Letters, A M Metaxis. O Howes' letter on giving blood is most interesting. Asians generally are most reluctant to give blood, thus in places like Malaysia, many Asians are kept alive by blood donated by Europeans.

During 18 years of observation, I have never noticed any deterioration in the racial purity of the Asians who are transfused with European blood.

Comment 1. The next day, the *SMH* had received so many Letters, that the Editor closed the correspondence. "Rarely have we received such a unanimous howl of protest."

Comment 2. He went on to raise an interesting point. "Few of our enlightened and indignant correspondents saw anything odd in Australia's readiness to accept the blood of Asians whom we do not allow to settle in the country."

A Post Script. Last year, **in 2014**, I conducted a meeting of 20 oldies who talked about their war-time and recent feelings about the Japanese. The next day **a pertinent letter arrived from Betty Nash.** It read:

Ron, I could not express myself last night, because I was overcome with emotion. I remembered how in 1943 my husband and his father were taken from our house in Malaya, (by Japanese), and shot dead in the dusty street outside. I was not able to speak last night.

This morning, I would like to say that I can appreciate the sentiments of most of the others at the meeting. It is good to forgive, and society is constantly telling us to do so. I appreciate that.

But I just can't do it. I never will. And to come to your question about accepting a blood transfusion from a Jap, I would never do this. I would die first.

Comment. I wonder now whether a few people at the meeting, who remained quiet, felt the same as Betty. I also wonder if the question had been put **in 1965, using Japanese as the potential donors**, would the response have been so one-sided? Or even now?

OUR NATIONAL ANTHEM AND ALL THAT

This first letter on this theme stirred up an interesting point, and got a large response.

Letters, C J Middleton. A few months ago, at a city cinema, I was rather surprised when a man did not stand while the national anthem was being played. I was even more surprised when the anthem was not played on the two occasions I attended the Sutherland-Williamson opera season.

I find that a number of theatres are not playing the national anthem. This is disgraceful. The anthem should be played, before, or after, all theatrical performances.

Letters, Michael Thomas. Rather than being shocked it would have been more appropriate if he had recognised the growing dissatisfaction among Australians, particularly the younger generations, concerning the institutional framework of Australian government.

First, we are called upon to declare our allegiance to a person whose residence is on the other side of the world. Secondly, and what I consider to be the more important, we have to stand for a "national" anthem that embodies nothing of Australian nationalism. Contrary to the Prime Minister's attitude, more and more people are becoming aware of this nationalism and the important role it has to play in Australia's future in this ever-changing region of the globe.

The anthem in its present state was significant when the British Commonwealth was a dynamic concept. However, this is now an ideal that is rapidly fading, irrespective of the two most recent attempts to bolster it up. The decline of the Commonwealth, especially in Asian affairs, was recently exemplified at the recent conference of the Conservative Party, where the "East of Suez" element in British policy was considered to be outmoded.

By blindly maintaining the status quo, we are not preparing for future eventualities and are in danger of finding ourselves in somewhat of a political void, with no national identity and with little resistance to American influence. This is not to say that all US policy should be automatically rejected simply because it is American, but that we should formulate our own policies according to our own situation. There is little doubt that the similarities will far outweigh the differences.

A tiny step in the right direction towards developing such a buffer would be a new anthem with a truly national content. More substantial steps might ensue from the further discussion on recommendations made by Mr Calwell, regarding the introduction of some form of Presidential system where the head of state is the true representative of the Australian people.

Letters, Leo Schofield. Poor C J Middleton! He may like to know that the national anthem isn't played at the Royal Opera House, Covent Garden, either – except at a Royal Gala. Not even when some member of the Royal family is there, having an informal night at the theatre. And lots of other theatres and cinemas in Britain don't play it either!

He may also like to know that the habit of sitting through the anthem is by no means uncommon in Britain, where people who do not care for the idea of royalty are not obliged to subscribe to the convention. Mr Middleton may stand if he cares to, but others can presumably choose for themselves.

I recently read a letter like Mr Middleton's in a London newspaper. The correspondent was making a similar point and complained angrily that, after standing patriotically rock-like through the anthem, at the end of it he found himself alone in the cinema... and locked in!

Letters, Ken Richards. What we need to do is avoid the spectacle in the United States where every trifling event is preceded by some sort of anthem. They stand there with their hands on their hearts, every one of them, apparently singing but really saying "we have been brainwashed, and we like it."

Comment. These Letters, entertaining enough, raised another important point. It was true that people were no longer responding to the anthem as they had in the past. As mentioned in one Letter, it was being played at fewer and fewer functions, and fewer people were standing for it, or waiting for it to finish. People were increasingly talking all the time it was being played.

These were not republicans who were protesting against our links to the monarchy, or to the paraphernalia that went with subservience to British. Most of them could just see no point to it. What did standing still prove? Some folk advocated saying a silent prayer at the time. What good would this prayer do, asked increasing numbers. Perhaps you could think of the power and glory of the British Empire. That seemed hardly likely, given the progressive dismemberment of the Empire or Commonwealth or whatever you called it now.

The point I am making is that most people were moving steadily towards the point of simply seeing no reason for such a shallow display of patriotism. They were genuine in their support for the nation, and indeed, for the Crown, but where was the need display it constantly, and what a silly way to do it.

Let me add that this almost-irreverence was part of a growing questioning of the nation's sacred cows. Aborigines were getting a more prolific and better Press. Women were moving into the workforce, for better or worse, and were moving towards goals like equal pay and opportunities. Our ties to Britain were breaking, and out international marketing efforts were paying off. It was a time when sacred cows were dying all round us.

HOW BAD ARE THE WHARFIES?

The wharfies lived a precarious life. They worked under a strange arrangement whereby they went to the wharves each morning, and then were told whether there would be work for them. If not, they went home, or hung round, hoping places would become available at a later shift. In some places, and at some times, life was a little better in that in the radio told them what the roster was before they turned out. But overall, it was still uncertain on a daily basis.

They did hard work, and it was also dangerous. Their work conditions were necessarily terrible, and they closely guarded every benefit that their Award and employers gave them. It was inevitable that disputes would occur about whether a certain job was safe to do, and whether it could be done at all according to the award. So strikes were happening at all wharfs regularly across the nation. Thus wharfies were unpopular with the general populace, and were constantly abused by the Press.

Now that the Federal Government was moving to make the wharfies Federation toe the line, part of the softening up process was to fling accusations at them claiming that they were all sorts of evil things, and would never be better, unless certain changes were accepted. This was par for the course, and was part of the normal give-and-take of industrial relations. But one particular accusation got a heated response.

Letters, (Mrs) I Jones, Balmain. As the wife of a waterside worker, I wish to say that I consider the statement of Mr McMahon that the Waterside Workers' Federation deliberately recruits criminals to the union one of the most irresponsible statements that a supposedly responsible member of Parliament and Minister could make.

How many employers of unskilled labour go into the records of every would-be employee to see if he has a police record, particularly large-scale industries? And even if he had, I believe most employers would be prepared to give him a job and a chance to earn a living, but the union must only take perfect men.

The watersiders' union has had the right to recruit labour for the last 60 years, and during two world wars, when, particularly during the last war, it was a very difficult job to get manpower and keep it working "round the clock" shifts.

Since the end of the war, because there is more work available, which makes the job a more stable one, large numbers of steady family men, a big percentage ex-Servicemen, and recently mostly young married men in their early twenties, have been attracted to the industry.

Their union has been democratically elected by these men. It is a militant union, and at present is leading the struggle against the misdeeds of the Federal Government, and that is the reason for the reckless and now vicious attacks on it by leaders of the Government.

Comment. I think it was widely accepted that the wharfies had their share of ex-criminals. The argument for this was that it was better for society that such men be gainfully employed than to leave them unemployed. It is a big argument that I will not enter into, but I do agree with Mrs Jones that it was a cheap shot by Mr McMahon.

MORE ON CRIMS AMONG WARFIES

Letters, P Stapleton. The political aspects of the dispute about the Waterside Workers' Federation aside, the present controversy criticising the number of employees on the waterfront with criminal records has done immeasurable harm to efforts to have Government and industry recognise **that once men have paid their penalties to society, they should be able once again to take virtually any job alongside those who haven't fallen foul of the law.**

It has been very difficult to get Government and industry of all kinds to recognise in practice the principle that once a man has paid his fine or has served a sentence for a crime, then he must be given every opportunity to rehabilitate both for his sake and for the sake of his family and the community at large.

It would be most regrettable indeed if Parliament and employing organisations were to be hustled into decisions that would adopt, in effect, the principle that, once convicted, a man should never have another chance of decent, regular job on good pay. If that is to be the case, our whole penal reform system is entirely useless, and we should admit it.

Comment. This is a question that has been raised over the years since then, and has never seen a societal consensus. It is being raised **at the moment, in 2019,** by vigilante groups who want to put paedophiles names on lists and publish the lists to alert citizens that they are among them. Whether such lists would be used to hound the ex-offender is a question that is hard to answer. **Should an offender who has served his time come back to society with a clean slate, so long as he does not re-offend? Can society take that risk?**

A PERENNIAL QUESTION

A *SMH* correspondent asked a question: Why was so much spent on Sydney's Waratah Festival when sheep in the country were dying from lack of food? Surely, she writes, the companies that provided floats could have instead payed to freight fodder from lush areas to areas of drought.

This is a question that consistently finds it way into the papers. No one ever tries to answer it, probably because there is no logical response. Granted the need for such fodder is great, but can city folk be expected to give up some luxury every time that country folk got into trouble? And vice versa?

The end result would be that people everywhere would have to give up everything all the time to help someone somewhere. Taking this point further, surely this would mean the introduction of the most severe form of Communism where all product would become the property of the State, and could be distributed as it willed. It seems to me, then, that this is a question without an answer. But that's only my opinion. What do you think?

NOVEMBER NEWS ITEMS

Dr H Evatt (Doc) died of pneumonia in his home in Canberra on November 2nd. He was aged 71. He had led an adventurous life and had won distinction as **Australia's youngest High Court judge, the President of the UN, and the leader of the Australian Labour Party.** He dropped out of politics about 5 years ago, after some difficulties with the Petrov affair. He will be given a State funeral.

US surgeons in Vietnam performed a bizarre operation this week. A South Vietnamese soldier had **a grenade fired into his back. It embedded there, and it did not explode.** US doctors arranged for a 10-foot wall of sandbags to be placed beside the man's bed, and it had a small window in it...

They then fixed a scalpel to 6-feet arms of steel, and looking through the small window, **proceeded to make an incision in his back, and then used long metal claws to remove the grenade.** It was safely disposed of.

Rhodesia, led by its white Premier, Ian Smith, seceded from the British Commonwealth. Britain did not agree with this. It was the first act of its kind since America declared its independence in 1776. The British Prime Minister, **Harold Wilson described it as "active, treasonable rebellion",** and imposed a number of trade and economic sanctions on the newly-independent nation.

Our casualties in Vietnam were growing. Over the weekend, two warrant officers were killed. The total now is **15 dead, and 85 wounded, and growing weekly.**

In NSW (and other States) **chocolate wheels, housiehousie, and raffles are illegal,** except with the hard-to-get permission of the Government. In practice, though, regulations stopping them are largely ignored. It seems likely that **these regulations will now be dropped.**

It seems likely that **suburban movie theatres will open on Sundays,** and also that **promoters will be able to charge entry fees for Sunday sport.** It is expected that **some Churches will battle hard to prevent these changes.**

The NSW Government will **take legal action against the directors of two companies that failed recently.** The companies are **Latec and IVM (International Vending Machines).** In both of these, and in newly-failed H G Palmer, very substantial **sums were lost by the general public who bought their debentures and notes, and IVM's franchises.**

In the US, a Government study asked whether **the use of the (contraceptive) pill damages the eyesight of users.** It was found to cause no defects, but the study was one of many attempts by conservative **groups to prevent usage of the pill.**

A huge dust storm engulfed Queensland and northern NSW as a result of the drought in Queensland. It was so bad that **sheep in the outback could not breathe, and thousands suffocated and died.**

A Sydney fisherman created **an Australian record for the catching of a tuna. The fish was 625 pounds,** and was 8 feet long, and 8 feet round the girth. It took the fisherman two and a half hours to land the fish.

Cricket lovers. A new recruit, **Doug Walters,** was chosen to play **his first Test match for Australia.** Walters, who is from the NSW country town of Dungog, is now aged 19.

Comment. I, a fervent cricketer and something of an expert, expect that Walters **will not have the experience nor the temperament to play big-time cricket,** and regretfully predict that he will be a flop, and will never be heard of again.

THE MELBOURNE CUP

The big race that I talked about was called the **Melbourne Cup**, and apparently it had become something of an annual event of note in Melbourne. **This year it was won by a horse, and I gather that this is not unusual.** I will not bother you with its name, because after all, the majority of readers are not in Melbourne, **and** it seems to be too late to get a bet on.

The real news from the Melbourne Cup was the appearance of Jean Shrimpton, **the Shrimp, in a mini dress**, a few inches above the knees. She also did not wear a hat. **Melbourne's society matrons were outraged**, and a nation-wide controversy erupted in protest at this display of immodesty. But the agitation was not all negative. She had as many bouquets as brickbats.

Was it proper for a young and beautiful woman to appear at a function thus dressed? For the next two days of the meeting, she did compromise by wearing slightly longer dresses, but still she wore no hat. She roundly attacked Melbourne society ladies on departure.

Her trip was not in vain. **The era of the mini-skirt started here in earnest as a consequence of her visit.**

CHEAP FIX FOR ABORIGINAL PROBLEMS

Mrs Faith Bandler was the NSW Secretary of the Federal Council for the Advancement of Aborigines. She, along with 35 other prominent Aborigines, is currently campaigning around Parliament for changes in the laws affecting Aborigines.

A census of the nation-wide electorate is soon to be conducted to perhaps have Aborigines counted in the national 5-year census. "People in Australia have to register their dogs and cats, but we do not know how many Aborigines there are".

She went on to say that "**For 4 million Pounds**, the cost of a modern jet bomber, we could solve most of the problems facing

Aborigines…. Without money, you will get bad housing, with bad housing you will get bad education, with bad education you will get poor employment."

Comment. Mrs Bandler had been prominent in the fight for Aborigines' rights for some time and had achieved much of value. Here, however, the sum of money she indicated would not scratch the surface, either in NSW or in Australia. So while it is easy to agree with her reasoning, we all know from experience that much more money would be called for.

CHILDREN DIE IN FRIDGE

A boy, aged 5, and a girl, aged 4, in a Sydney suburb, died yesterday when they were locked into an empty fridge. They were playing, and they climbed into the fridge, which closed on them. They would have suffocated in about 10 minutes.

CHURCHES, CONSCIES, AND DISSONANCE

Whenever **threatened-warfare becomes a reality**, there is always a part of the community that says the nation should **not** take up arms. When Hitler in 1938 began his takeovers of adjacent countries, Britain was torn by division over when and if it should intervene. By the time WWII was underway, and Japan attacked Australia, however, almost all Australians **agreed that we must defend ourselves**.

On the other hand, when it came to Korea, and when it was not clear that we were in any danger, the population here was luke-warm in acceptance of intervention. So much so, that now that it is over, it is widely recognised as the "forgotten war."

At the moment, a war was clearly brewing in Vietnam. We already had forces in Vietnam masquerading as advisers and technical assistants, and our men were being killed. Such deaths can normally be counted on to provoke a population into fervour in favour of strong action, but in this case, here in Australia, **enthusiasm for another war was, at the most, tepid**. Thus, there were constant marches in the streets protesting against the fighting in Vietnam, and the papers were full of written protests.

Also, **when war became a reality**, and young men were forced to take up arms, there were some among them who did not want to. Some of these were **genuinely ideologically or religiously opposed to war**, some were opposed to this particular war, and others simply did not want anything to do with killing, or with the military, or with fighting. In any case, when it came to a military call-up, these protestors said they were **conscientious objectors**, and the military authorities decided **how** ideologically genuine their concerns were, and then exempted some of them from the fighting ranks, even though they were made to serve in other capacities. The derogatory term for these was "**conscies**", and in the two World Wars, it was a term of contempt.

The Victorian General Assembly of the Presbyterian Church decided that its ministers should **give practical support to its church members who wished to avoid fighting**. It agreed that it had supported fighting service in all wars in the past, but **that this time the situation was different**. It could see that the general public was not supportive, that the Labour Party was explicitly negative, that it was believed that some North Vietnam forces were being tortured by our allies, and that the young men being conscripted were not yet old enough to vote. **It was a curious grab-bag of reasons**, but the Assembly agreed on that basis to help church members who wanted to avoid being called-up, and also those who were called-up and wanted to avoid fighting.

Letter, Brian Dunlop. My son was recently called-up. He is a genuine pacifist. I do not agree with him. I think that we cannot pick and choose what we fight for, and that if the national government in this democracy decides we should go to war, we stop arguing and do what is needed. But he has been a long-term pacifist for years, so I respect his views, and I will try as hard as he does to avoid his engagement in this war.

On the other hand, I do object to my local clergyman saying from the pulpit on Sunday that he is prepared to give a reference stating that any youth called up could come to the manse and **get a signed letter saying he was regular churchgoer and also a long term pacifist**. He would use this to press his claim before any Board who would judge his claim to avoid service.

If this is the "practical support" that the Church envisages, and I think it is, I think the Church needs to think again.

Be that as it may, there were plenty of organisations who agreed with the spirit of avoidance. Little groups resistant to the war and conscription sprang up everywhere, especially when it was seen that some Churches were prepared to go down the same path.

Letters, C McLean, Sec, Objectors to Conscription Advisory Cttee. It is heartening to read the "Herald's" front-page story on October 15 on the decision of the Victorian Presbyterian General Assembly to give practical support to their young members who are conscientious objectors to Army conscription.

Many young men are unaware of their legal rights under the National Service Act, which allows them to declare themselves conscientious objectors for religious or humanitarian reasons.

We would hope that other denominations would make similar decisions to support their 20-year-old members who make this choice – or to refer them to the Objectors to Conscription Advisory Committee, 5 Hainsworth Street, Westmead, which was set up in NSW to inform young men of their rights and the procedure necessary to establish themselves as conscientious objectors.

Comment. Public opinion remained divided, and confusion reigned supreme. These were many people who, unlike the Victorian Presbyterians, thought that conscies were ducking their duty, and thus disapproved of them. But a large number thought that **this** almost-war was not a battle that we should be in. So the propaganda on both sides was starting to ratchet up.

Some supporters of intervention brought in unusual arguments.

Letters, James Duncan. If the Presbyterian Church continues with the move to give practical support to conscientious objects, it would appear that this Church has lost sight of its mission. In every country, without exception, which has fallen to Communism, religious liberty has been ruthlessly suppressed.

Today the fight for freedom is being waged in South Vietnam, and if this battle is lost, religious liberty will be lost with it in yet another part of the world.

It is noteworthy that in South Vietnam this year, Christian and non-Christian religious bodies alike joined together to form the Citizens of Different Confessions. Among their objectives they said they would:

"One. Fight with all our might for independence, freedom and democracy in the country; and

"Two. Defend energetically and at all costs the freedom and equality of all religions."

It would seem more in keeping with the mission of the Presbyterian Church if it were to turn its energies to the defence of religious freedom wherever it is threatened.

As well as that, there were the arguments based on religion..

Letters, (Rev) John D Ross. James Duncan is very mistaken in his view of the mission of the Presbyterian Church. Yes, of course, we are interested in defending religious freedom, but we're even more worried about freedom for individuals, and this is why we are trying to see that conscientious objectors get a fair hearing.

You see the head of our Church is Jesus Christ Himself (not SEATO) and He gives us some very disturbing advice. He tells us that he who saves his life will lose it! And if the Presbyterian Church tries only to perpetuate and protect itself as a prop of any power group, then it's lost its mission altogether, and will fold up. And rightly so.

Rather our Church's job is to show something of the power of God's concern for all men and women. We try to help our young people grow up in a world of power blocs and prejudice. I don't see how we can do this by deserting them when they seriously question the aims and methods of war – or when they take more seriously than we may the teachings of Jesus Himself.

Indeed, by this very decision, our Church is showing herself very concerned about this huge problem of peace and freedom. We know there's no easy solution – but Jesus was interested in peace and freedom too!

Comment. As the war became "official", and as our deaths and involvement grew larger, the forces for and against involvement at all levels increased. Over the next year, 1966, dissension grew and the nation lost its long-time air of complacency, and for a while this country saw more dissonance than we had seen for a long, long time

There was plenty to argue about. I give you two fervent Letters as examples of what was to come.

Letters, J G Stead. I am urged to write in the face of growing Press and public comment inferring that those who fail to support Australian participation in the Vietnam war are unpatriotic. I wish to take issue and assert that this is not so, feeling as I do that the Australian forces should be withdrawn at the earliest possible date.

During the last war, at the time when an invasion was considered imminent, I worked directly as part of a secret organisation training civilians to ensure that no major or minor resources of our country fell intact to the Japanese military forces.

During the week, I have discussed this matter with three men who were personally responsible to me, and each of them supports the view that Australian participation is wrong. A withdrawal would be a concrete step towards peaceful settlement and thus directly serve the best interests of our country.

NOVEMBER 129

Australian foreign policy ignores the fact that we people a continent located in Asia. Necessity demands that this be recognised.

Letters, Douglas McPherson. Over the past 20 years many a German arraigned before the tribunal of history has given as his defence that he did not know what was going on. Had he done so he would not have supported the Nazi regime.

We Australians have been co-opted to support American policy and American actions in Vietnam. Shall we be able to stand before some future tribunal and make the same defence? I think not, for occasional American military blunders reveal the hidden truths.

Once again the American Air Force has strafed a friendly village in mistake for one under the control of the Vietcong. A justifiable mistake, doubtless, from a military point of view.

But the lesson to be learned seems perfectly plain: the bombing of villages and the killing of civilians is routine to American military adventuring in that most unhappy country.

Such actions also explain the fury with which the Vietcong succeeded in breaking through American defences to destroy some 48 planes on the ground.

Comment. The Vietnam story still had a long way to go.

SACRED SUNDAYS

Various moves to put some **life into Sundays** were opposed every inch of the way by some churches. Three clergymen, writing separately, provided strong Letters on the virtues of preserving Sundays as days of prayer and contemplation.

They wrote that, as the matter now stood, Sundays were times where families and neighbours and indeed, the whole community, could quietly come together in a fellowship, and calmly evaluate the world they occupied in a Christian spirit.

It provided the opportunity for those with a practicing faith to congregate and share their fellowship in a forum that enhanced their relationship with God, and encouraged all persons to think about the welfare of the rest of society.

The underlying tenets of Sunday observance are simply that people should not pursue their commercial interests any more than the needs of society demanded. Thus, they could work on essential services, or perform works of charity. Further, that entertainment in any form should not be organised on a large scale, and that meant there could be no admission fees for Sunday sport or concerts.

The writers were fearful that recent moves by governments, allowing for a few sports to charge even token admissions, would be the thin edge of the wedge, and that soon all sports would be demanding the right to charge and that would put an end to Sundays' sanctity. The idea of Sunday given to contemplation and fellowship would give way to Sunday spent racing to play or watch sports played before large crowds and sometimes hysterical parents. The whole idea of the traditional Sunday would be lost.

The disruption would go further than that. The generation of crowds would mean that many persons, who were quite content with a contemplative Sunday, would be forced to work to accommodate such crowds. Further, some players would be excluded from teams because of their preference for sanctity and holiness, and that would not be fair to them nor to their teams.

Finally, they concluded, the governments had no mandate from the people to make such changes, and it was to be hoped they would not do so.

These Letters elicited a response from a C J S Purdy, who was a well-known columnist and master of all things relating to chess. He pointed out that no one was forced to work on Sundays, and that those who did were well payed for doing so.

He, along with other writers, argued that in a democracy, persons were free to make their own choices. If some wanted to play sport, they should be free to do so. If others wanted religion, have it by all means. If, in some cases these wants clashed, then the individual had a choice to make.

But do not compel every one to a single course of action. In this case do not force a large majority to follow the way of a small minority. Do not let the tail wave the dog.

THE PILL AGAIN

I mentioned earlier that some conservative groups were opposed to anybody using the contraceptive pill. Still, more and more women were switching to it, even though no one was sure that it would not have long-term bad effects on users. Despite many assurances that it was perfectly safe, its opponents were vociferous in their exaggerated claims in opposition to it.

Now the Australian Minister for Health weighed in, and said that a small decrease in the nation's fertility rate was being caused by the pill. This might or might not have been true, or the drop might or might not have been caused by small statistical variations, or by hot or cold weather, and so on. No one could know at this early stage.

Letters, (Mrs) Z Fuad. I fail to see why the fall in Australia's birthrate is seen by the NSW Minister for Health, Mr A H Jago, as a "national tragedy."

What would have been the merit of bringing into our community those unborn babies who, presumably, **were unborn for a valid reason?** A fair percentage of them would have arrived with an unfair start in life, insecure, unwanted or illegitimate.

Surely Mr Jago knows that no quantity of contraceptive pills will ever quench the most forceful urge in the majority of women, her maternal instinct. She will have as many children as she wants. Why, then, blame the pill for discouraging the less maternal, who don't want any children, or who find a small family adequate, when they are unable emotionally or financially to cope?

Of course Australia needs more people; our pathetically small population on this vast continent makes us a weak nation. Why do we not boost our migration intake of adults, who can be working for the country's progress (which today's babies cannot do for at least 20 years) and still contribute to the birthrate with their children.

Please, Mr Jago, don't reduce our prime function in life to being little more than brood mares.

Letters, (Mrs) J Hutchinson. I feel that "Protestant Mother" is to be pitied. The poor woman obviously has a strong persecution complex.

I have been taking the Pill for over two years now, and as I have moved to different suburbs, I have had my prescription renewed by several doctors. **Never once have I experienced moral, or any other type of bullying.**

I must confess that I have often been kept waiting in chemists' shops, but it has never occurred to me to wonder if the pharmacists were Catholic, Protestant or Mormons. In my ignorance I have assumed that my wait was because other prescriptions were in the process of being made up.

Letters, Alan Burke. I go to the chemist once a month for pills for my heart aliment. He always keeps me waiting for twenty minutes.

Can anyone tell me what religion he is?

Letters, F M Godbold. Mr Swartz, Federal Minister for Health, advises women to take oral contraceptive pills only under medical advice. The point which Mr Swartz overlooks is that of thousands of people **suffering from side-effects of the pill** all took the pill under medical supervision.

If a doctor prescribed the pill it would do just as much harm as if it was prescribed by a herbalist. The only way to avoid the harmful effects of any drug is not to take it. There are many safe and effective contraceptive methods available without taking unnecessary risks with our health.

DECEMBER NEWS ITEMS

The Post Office is changing over to decimal currency. From next February, the nation's stamps will show the price in cents. A series of 12 stamps were exhibited this week, and show birds, fish and a hermit crab. There will also be three designs showing Queen Elizabeth.

Surprise, surprise. **The cost of building the Sydney Opera House will rise by seven million Pounds to 24 million.**

The price of **a packet of 12 Bex powders** will increase from 1 Shilling to one Shilling and Threepence.

The Federal Government is getting jumpy. A number of people have been telling them that our balance of trade is suffering, and that the internal economy is slowing down. Now, it has announced that **more credit will be released** for home loans, and that more releases will follow soon. Sure signs that **our leaders are starting to worry**.

A young couple had **a simple, inconspicuous, wedding on Saturday in Melbourne**. They were Diana Knox, reported as the **richest girl in Australia**, and Adrian Gibson, son of Justice Gibson of Tasmania....

Among the guests were the Governor General, the Victorian Premier, Mr Holt the Federal Treasurer, Melbourne's Lord Mayor, the former Governor of Victoria, several Lords and Ladies, and many Members of Parliament and clergy. The ceremony was performed by the Bishop of Tasmania.

Canberra Theatre Trust has just opened a new theatre complex, and **a concert hall for 1,200**. It is open for bookings. However, **it has refused booking for concerts by Tom Jones, and Herman and the Hermits....**

The trust says that **it must refuse bookings** "for any attraction in which **the aim of the performers is to stir up a teenage**

audience to movement in and around seats. Our seating is of very light construction, and such concerts might prejudice the use of the theatre on the following day"….

Harry Miller, of Pan-Pacific Promotions, said that he has promoted many concerts in all the major venues round Australia, and **has never had complaints about damage to the theatre or seating**. He is appealing, but even if successful, the concerts due in February will not be approved.

Federal Minister for Labour, **Billie McMahon was married in Sydney on December 10ᵗʰ**. He later became Prime Minister. **His wife, nee Sonya** Hopkins, also attended the ceremony, and **later became famous for That Dress.**

Doug Walters, mentioned earlier, playing in his first Test match against England, **made a century. He made 119 not out** at the end of the day's play. It is wonderful to see such a brilliant batsman come onto the scene, and I am happy to say that, while a few commentators thought he would fail, **I never doubted him for a minute.**

"Mia Farrow has had her long locks cut off." The **lead-story** in the Sun-Herald newspaper on Sunday 19ᵗʰ December.

Two convicts on the run after escaping from Pentridge Gaol on December 20ᵗʰ **killed a warder in the course of their escape.** One of the escapees is Ronald Ryan who, when eventually captured, **was the last man executed in Oz.**

Back to where we started. Early in the year, **Indonesia and Malaysia were at each others throats**, and were having their small skirmishes around their borders. Later, Indonesia was preoccupied while President Soekarno had troubles with some of his Red generals, and he had them executed. Now, his off-siders said that the **confrontation will continue with new vigour.** Oh goody, just what the region needs.

1965 AMERICAN FILMS

SOUND OF MUSIC	JULIE ANDREWS
DR ZHIVAGO	OMAR SHARIF, JULIE CHRISTIE
THUNDERBALL	SEAN CONNERY
THE GREAT RACE	TONY CURTIS, JACK LEMMON
CAT BALLOU	JANE FONDA, LEE MARVIN
WHAT'S NEW, PUSSTCAT?	PETER SELLERS, PETER O'TOOLE
THE SANDPIPER	ELIZABETH TAYLOR, RICHARD BURTON
SONS OF KATIE ELDER	JOHN WAYNE, DEAN MARTIN
HELP	THE BEATLES
THE AGONY AND ECSTASY	CHARLTON HESTON
SPY CAME FROM COLD	RICHARD BURTON,
DO NOT DISTURB	DORIS DAY, ROD TAYLOR
A PATCH OF BLUE	SIDNEY POITIER,

1965 HIT PARADE

I Can't Get No Satisfaction	Rolling Stones
Mr Tambourine Man	The Byrds
Help	Beatles
Yesterday	Beatles
Ticket to Ride	Beatles
A World of Our Own	The Seekers
As Tears Go By	Marianne Faithful
Downtown	Petula Clark
The Sound of Silence	Simon, Garfunkel
Barbara Ann	The Beach Boys
Zorba the Greek	Herb Alpert, Tijuanna Brass
I Got You Babe	Sonny and Cher
Like a Rolling Stone	Bob Dylan
Stop! In the Name of Love	The Supremes
What's New Pussycat?	Tom Jones

TIDYING UP VIETNAM

The major story of the year has been the increasing level of war in Vietnam. I have deliberately kept the coverage down to a fairly low level, but I am confident that you would have realised what a growing menace it was. I hope you also got the message that there were no clear-cut goodies and baddies there. Rather it was a contest between Capitalism and Communism, being orchestrated by people who were far removed from any actual hostilities.

Australia had entered the war in 1962, but only with advisers and the like. By 1965, we were getting more serious, and that year saw 16 Australians killed, and hundreds seriously wounded. Overall, from 1962 to its end, **the war took the lives of 480 servicemen, with 3,000 wounded**.

From the start of 1966, opposition in Oz society to the war increased from the levels we have seen up to a much higher level. This opposition increased hugely when Government said that **the 20-year-old conscripts, the nashos, were to be sent into the fray**. Every mum and dad and all their relatives and friends now got involved. What was the reason for sending our young lads off to their death? Was it so big a threat, up there somewhere in Asia, that we needed to kill our own youngsters? Dissension grew and public demonstrations, many of them ugly, divided the nation till our war ended in 1972.

Note that 190 Nashos were killed in action in the war.

In case anyone does not remember the overall outcome, let me remind you that the Americans pulled out after 1972, and South Vietnam and also Laos and Cambodia were over-run by the Vietcong.

Final comment. When will we ever learn?

NO PEERAGE FOR MENZIES

There were currently many commentators who thought that Prime Minister Menzies would soon leave the Australian political scene, and that he would be granted a peerage from the Queen. A precedent had been set for this by **Lord Stanley Bruce**. This latter gentleman had been Australia's eighth Prime Minister from 1923 to 1929, and had subsequently held senior positions in Australia and Britain until his death in 1967. **In 1947, he was granted a peerage**, and thereby entry to Britain's House of Lords.

So it was possible that Menzies might follow in his footsteps into that hallowed institution. Recently, however, Menzies had bought a house in Melbourne, and that suggested that he was not looking for a House in London. Now, he had been given the title of Lord Warden of the Cinque Ports, and although it sounded great, and was a genuine honour, it was not the same as a peerage. In fact, it was generally seen as indicating that this was as far as he would go, and probably, that Melbourne in fact was as far as he wanted to go.

Be that as it may, a few writers had their say on his movements. The Herald lead writer was hardly congratulatory. He asked "Why on Earth is our Prime Minister paddling in the English Channel?" He added "The Warden of the Cinque Ports is a proud title for any man, but does it not devalue, if only infinitesimally, the far prouder title of Prime Minister of Australia?"

With that ringing endorsement, lesser writers added their bit.

Letters, Mrs Y Rentoul. Of all the constant anti-Menzies editorials published in your paper, your comments on Mr Menzies last Friday must surely take the accolade for blind prejudice and infantile reasoning.

Letters, Josh McRae. To the Editor. I was caught up with the romance and glamour of the new Menzies title.

But thanks to your great wisdom and smart-alec writing, I can now see that he should never have accepted that position, and must surely keep his mind firmly on doing the job that we pay him for. We are lucky to have your pragmatic advice to stop us romancing.

CHRISTMAS CHEER

I have been writing these books for twelve years. This is my 27th in the series, and by now I sometimes get the feeling that no Oz development of any sort will surprise me. But now, right near the finish of my writing career, I have indeed been **surprised by the editorial policy** of the Sydney Morning Herald. Let me explain.

At this time of the year, the *SMH* always does its best to lift Christmas sales by cutting back on **its normal routine of stories of horror, despair, and impending doom**. Instead, it drops most of its coverage of such matters, and fills its pages with lighter stuff. So that as we get closer to Christmas, we get more and more stories about Christmas, and the season of good-will.

Thus we hear matrons complaining about the crush on trains, and the lack of proper sacred music in the shops. Others complain about the commercialisation of Christmas, and the lack of religion in displays. Crowds are considered bad, prices have risen, excessive eating and drinking is deplored, and Chrissie office parties are excuses for sinful behaviour. No wonder so many ladies fainted in the pushing and shoving at the perfume counter.

Reading all of this is quite entertaining, even though sometimes it just reminds me of **how many nutters there are in society**.

This year, though, it is different. **The Herald carried not a single reference to any of the above.** It must have held back the normal avalanche of Letters, and chosen to publish a different collection altogether.

Some of these Letters are shown below. **All of them relate to the rapidly changing retail trade.** You will find as you read them that many of them are touching on issues that, starting then, have grown steadily over the years and are still being played out in our shops today.

Letters, Norman Tieck, Managing Director, Franklins Food Stores, Turramurra. The front-page article "Retailers uncover dishonest staff" rendered the community a valuable service in highlighting the alarming wave of dishonesty which is currently plaguing the retail trade.

Perhaps the real significance of the article lies in how this dishonesty is affecting the cost of living. Retailers are incurring very heavy costs in trying to check dishonesty in its various forms of shoplifting, pilferage by staff, robbery by manufacturers' deliverymen, and organised burglary on a substantial scale.

We at Franklins estimate that, if these different forms of dishonesty could be reduced, the average family grocery bill of 5 Pounds a week could be lessened by 5/. In other words, the great majority of honest people are paying 5/ a week to maintain the small minority in their nefarious practices.

The Police Force today, obviously overworked and undermanned, is simply not able to cope with the big job of eliminating crime in the food industry. We retailers are doing our best to do so; meanwhile, the money we are losing comes out of housewives' purses.

Letters, M Jones. We, the general public, scarcely know the right price or fair price of many of the articles we buy today. There is so much 'discounting' going on. For a "trade-in" we are offered 30 Pounds here, 50 Pounds at another place and 80 Pounds somewhere else and so we thrash about until we think we've got the cheapest price offering. We have seen such ridiculous "reductions" of 10 pounds off for a rusty iron or so much off for a clothes-peg. Sometimes the "trade-in" is accepted, sometimes we can take it to the nearest tip so far as the firm is concerned.

Perhaps the retail traders would enlighten us on why this trend has been allowed to develop. Is it regarded as honest trading or horse-trading or are retailers helping to cut their own throats?

Letters, Walter Bass. The ever changing shapes, sizes and features of manufactured articles, often changed at the expense of performance, the blatant examples of built-in obsolescence, the ridiculous prices of spare parts and repairs; all this has done untold harm to the manufacturer's image in the public eye.

Smooth talking, irresponsible salesmen using the "only a few shillings a week" routine to talk people into buying articles they cannot possibly afford have caused a very understandable resentment on the part of the buyers who realise only when they receive their contracts that they have entered into a commitment they cannot possibly honour. Many of these salesmen use selling tactics which make refusal almost impossible for the timid client.

The noisy, insistent, often misleading advertising campaigns blasting the public ear and eye from every direction must surely be expected to cause a counter-reaction and there are many signs that this relentless selling campaign is creating a race of cynical, disbelieving buyers, while at the same time robbing the English language of most of its meaning. Constant use of nonsensical pseudo-statistics of the "37 per cent brighter and 25 per cent stronger" variety, and the never-ending flow of "NEW IMPROVED" products that turn out to be the old one in a different box, these gimmicks are taking their toll of the public patience.

Who can blame the buyer, constantly subjected to campaigns falsely offering him something for nothing, if he tries to turn this original mirage into a reality? This is not a weakening of the public morals, but rather a case of the worm turning!

Letters, A Roberts. Owner-managed stores which have survived are by the very nature of things more efficient than those employing paid managers. Owners count things, they watch things, they examine things, they constantly devise new methods, new checks – they watch the till rather than the clock.

That is why on a straight value-for-money comparison, they compare very favourably indeed with the most efficient chains, and **are in the process of earning their way back into public favour**, as they have already done overseas.

Letters, N Tieck, Franklins Stores, Turramurra. Over 2,000 "small" groceries went out of business between 1957 and 1962 – and the trend has accelerated since.

This, of course, is highly regrettable. But one of the facts of life in the grocery trade today – hard as it may seem – is that business has become increasingly competitive and only efficiently managed stores are surviving.

It is an equally valid fact that, by virtue of its greater efficiency, the chain store usually knows what is going on in its own business. If those small owner-managed stores which have gone out of business had known better what was going on, they would probably have survived.

Comment. I thought about how many small stores had gone from my own childhood town of Abermain in the NSW coalfields. This was a town of 2,000 people.

My recollection is that three grocery stores are missing. Suffering the same fate are a butcher, two barbers, a blacksmith, a milk-bar, as well as home-delivery men such as two bakers, a fruit-o, an insurance collector, a travelling Chinaman, a rabbit-o, and a clothes-prop and radio-aerial man.

All readers will have their own lists. Collectively, when taken with the motor car, they reflect **a major social change** in the way we do our shopping, and our interacting with other people. Of course **we all decry the loss of the corner store, but** somewhere in all of us, I think we still like **the current one-stop shopping**, and the big array of goods, and the cleanness and service that the supermarkets bring.

SUMMING UP 1965

When I was writing up the conclusions for each of the war years, I had little of encouragement until 1944. Prior to then, it was easy to see that the next few years might be a lot worse. Even in 1944, when the Nazis were on the run, there was always the uncertainty that maybe, somehow, they could recover, and turn the tables. But also, for those with loved ones still in the armed forces, there was always the real fear that **deaths were certain to occur**. It was hard for me to be at all cheery about the future under those circumstances.

After that, the later years were just a procession of brighter and brighter prospects. For this nation, the economy kept improving, families kept forming, jobs were always available, houses could be scrimped for and then bought. For all the problems that the poorer people experienced, we could always point overseas to many others there who were worse off. So, when I came to the end of a year, I could always say to people born that year that they were lucky for that very reason, and that things looked even better next year.

At the end of 1965, though, I have my doubts. There is a real shadow hanging over the nation. I have already told you about the Vietnam war, and that 3,500 boys would be killed or wounded. You don't need to be told that these boys are real, living, vibrant, silly, fun-filled boys who will not be the same again. Nor that others will come back with no physical injuries, but with equivalent psychological damage, and they will never be the same again, either. This is the shadow I see, and it will loiter as a shadow till 1972 and beyond.

Apart from that, there is some real action about to come strongly to the fore. **The Aborigines** are starting to agitate on a more organised basis, and will soon get legislative improvements to their status and conditions. **Women**, partially due to the freedom from the pill, are making their voices heard more and more, though they still lack organisations and philosophies that speak with united voices. Betty Friedan (*The Feminine Mystique*) and Germaine Greer (*The Female Eunuch*) were just around the corner, though. In any case, I think that women are very likely here to stay.

In other matters, like the internal economy and jobs and housing and Sunday barbeques, and Hills Hoists, the situation will continue on as it has for almost two decades, almost like a dream that is too good to be true. Next year, our international terms of trade will probably tighten, but we can and will shrug that off. For most of the population next year, and the year after, and on into the future, looks about as good as it can get.

So, if you were born in 1965, it looks like you were off to a pretty good start. The first few years would be unsettled, due to Vietnam, but after that, blue skies for most of you for most of the time. For those of you who had more than your fair share of grey skies in that period, I would say that at least the nation around you at those times has been a great one to live in, and the **forty years** without any **major** wars has stopped other, worse considerations from adding to your woes.

For you, and the many readers of my 32 books, no matter what year you were born, I hope **above all else** that those **forty years turn into 400**, and that you all survive and prosper for many of those years.

COMMENTS FROM READERS

Tom Lynch, Spears Point.....Some history writers make the mistake of trying to boost their authority by including graphs and charts all over the place. You on the other hand get a much better effect by saying things like "he made a pile". Or "every one worked hours longer than they should have, and felt like death warmed up at the end of the shift." I have seen other writers waste two pages of statistics painting the same picture as you did in a few words....

Barry Marr, Adelaide....you know that I am being facetious when I say that I wish the war had gone on for years longer so that you would have written more books about it...

Edna College, Auburn.... A few times I stopped and sobbed as you brought memories of the postman delivering letters, and the dread that ordinary people felt as he neared. How you captured those feelings yet kept your coverage from becoming maudlin or bogged down is a wonder to me....

Betty Kelly. Every time you seem to be getting serious you throw in a phrase or memory that lightens up the mood. In particular, in the war when you were describing the terrible carnage of Russian troops, you ended with a ten line description of how aggrieved you felt and finished with "apart from that, things are pretty good here". For me, it turned the unbearable into the bearable, and I went from feeling morbid and angry back to a normal human being....

Alan Davey, Brisbane....I particularly liked the light-hearted way you described the scenes at the airports as the American high-flying entertainers flew in. I had always seen the crowd behaviour as disgraceful, but your light-hearted description of it made me realise it was in fact harmless and just good fun....

In 1953, pets in churches were welcomed with open arms. Painless childbirth was popular, especially among women. Be warned - the coronation of Elizabeth will soon be in the news. Edmund Hillary reached the top. Thallium became popular, as a footballer found out. Lots of Pom migrants had done their time, and went back to Mother England.

In 1954, Queen Elizabeth II was sent here victorious, and Petrov was our very own spy - what a thrill. Boys were being sentenced to life. Johnny Ray cried all the way to the bank. Church halls were being used for dirty dancing. Open the pubs after six? Were they ever shut? A-bombs had scaredies scared.

****

Chrissi and birthday books for Mum and Dad and Aunt and Uncle and cousins and family and friends and work and everyone else.

Don't forget a good read and chuckle for yourself.

In 1947, Labor was still in power, but would not give motorists much petrol until 1950. The Poms were firing rockets over our Aborigines, while Menzies was discovering Reds under our Beds. Our new Governor General was not a Pom, but a local lad, and Princess Elizabeth said yes to a Greek. Six boys under 17 were gaoled for life for rape, and 10 o'clock closing might stop the six o'clock swill. Indonesia, India and Israel wanted the colonials to go, and cricket was again thriving on on-field hatred of the Poms. Most of our foreign travel was still done by great big overseas liners. These were striking times.

In 1948, there was no shortage of rationing and regulation, as the Labor government tried to convince voters that war-time restrictions should stay. The concept of free medicine was introduced, but doctors (still controlled from Britain) would not co-operate, so that medicines on the cheap were scarcely available to the public. Immigration Minister Calwell was staunchly supporting our White Australia Policy, though he would generously allow five coloured immigrants from each Asian nation to settle here every year. Burials on Saturday were banned. Rowers in Oxford were given whale steak to beat meat rationing.

In 1956, the first big issue was the Suez crisis, which put our own Bob Menzies on the world stage, but he got no applause. TV was turned on in time for the Melbourne Olympics, Hungary was invaded and the Iron Curtain got a lot thicker. There was much concern about cruelty to sharks, and the horrors of country pubs persisted. No nation came out of the Suez crisis with any honour.

****

AVAILABLE FROM ALL GOOD BOOK STORES

AND NEWSAGENTS